# Edexcel | AS | UNIT 2

# Economics

## Managing the Economy

Rachel Cole

Philip Allan Updates, an imprint of Hodder Education, an Hachette UK Company, Market Place, Deddington, Oxfordshire, OX15 0SE

**Orders**
Bookpoint Ltd, 130 Milton Park, Abingdon, Oxfordshire, OX14 4SB
tel: 01235 827720
fax: 01235 400454
e-mail: uk.orders@bookpoint.co.uk
Lines are open 9.00 a.m.–5.00 p.m., Monday to Saturday, with a 24-hour message answering service. You can also order through the Philip Allan Updates website: www.philipallan.co.uk

ISBN 978-0-340-94798-2

First printed 2008
Impression number  9  8  7
Year  2013  2012  2011  2010

This Guide has been written specifically to support students preparing for the Edexcel AS Economics Unit 2 examination. The content has been neither approved nor endorsed by Edexcel and remains the sole responsibility of the author.

Typeset by Phoenix Photosetting, Chatham, Kent
Printed by MPG Books, Bodmin

Hachette Livre UK's policy is to use papers that are natural, renewable and recyclable products and made from wood grown in sustainable forests. The logging and manufacturing processes are expected to conform to the environmental regulations of the country of origin.

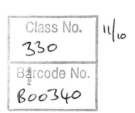

# Contents

## Introduction

■ ■ ■

## Content Guidance

■ ■ ■

## Questions and Answers

# Introduction

## Aims

This guide has been written to prepare students for Unit 2 of Edexcel's Advanced Subsidiary (AS) GCE examinations in economics. It provides an overview of the knowledge and skills required to achieve a high grade in the examination for 'Managing the Economy'. The unit's main emphasis is on the issues associated with measures of economic performance, income and wealth, aggregate demand and supply, and macroeconomic policy in the UK.

In preparing for your revision programme (a process which itself should be allowed an hour or two), organise your notes in line with the major topics presented in this guide. Here are the topics, together with a summary of the issues involved.

(1) **Measuring the performance of countries.** As an introduction to economics, we look at a range of ways in which we can assess the economic performance of a country. Economics is a study of the management of resources, and *macroeconomics* looks at indicators at an aggregate or total level. For example, in Unit 2 we do not look at the individual pricing decisions of a firm or consumer, but at all the prices in the economy. We do not focus on whether one person's wage will make him or her unemployable, but consider wages and employment levels throughout the economy.

(2) **Income and wealth.** In this section we introduce a simple way of understanding the macroeconomy: as a circular flow of income. The causal relationships between income and spending, spending and output, and output and income make up the circle. In this context we can understand how injections and leakages will alter the flow and have a significant macroeconomic impact.

(3) **Aggregate demand and supply.** These are the forces which together determine the price level and equilibrium real output in the economy. We examine what causes these to shift and the likely impact on the macroeconomy.

(4) **Economic growth — causes, constraints and costs.** Using aggregate demand and supply analysis, we can give reasons for changes in the rate of economic growth, and indicate some of the likely side-effects.

(5) **Macroeconomic objectives of governments.** This section brings the government into the picture of how the economy functions.

(6) **Policy instruments.** The tools that the government uses to try to influence the macroeconomy are explained, and their functions and likely side-effects are examined. It becomes apparent that in trying to improve some aspects of the economy, other aspects are also affected, sometimes for the better but often for the worse.

## How to use this guide

This guide is aimed at developing your AS skills, and should be used alongside your notes and other revision aids. The guide includes typical questions and answers, and explains what the examiners are looking for. Common mistakes are highlighted and several strategies for increasing your marks are suggested.

This introduction explains the format of the examination paper and the skills that will be tested. It also provides useful tips on revision planning and sitting the examination. A final 4-week revision programme for Unit 2 is also included.

The Content Guidance section provides an overview of the main topics, identifying what has to be learnt and explaining the theoretical requirements of the unit.

The final part of the guide provides questions and answers on the economic concepts and topics in Unit 2. There are four data-response questions covering the main topic areas, with a selection of student answers to give you an idea of the level of answer required to achieve a grade A. The answers are interspersed with examiner's comments — a helpful way of getting to know the expectations of those who will mark your papers. After reviewing the Unit 2 topics, you should try these sample questions, ideally under timed conditions, and then compare your work with the answers and comments provided. This will allow you to identify areas of weakness that require further work.

## Examination format

Unit 2 makes up 50% of the total marks in the AS examination (25% of the A-level). It is worth a maximum of 100 UMS marks. (UMS stands for the 'uniform mark system', which scales your actual mark to one that by statistical correction makes it equivalent to any other exam.) You will need to answer one question from a choice of two data-response questions, including a final mini-essay worth 30 marks, with total marks adding up to 80.

As a rough guide to the standard required, for the June 2007 examinations the A-grade boundary for the old Unit 3 was set at an equivalent of 58/80, grade C at 42/80 and grade E at 28/80. A raw score of 74/80 scored full marks on the uniform system. However, you should be aware that these grade thresholds change according to the examiners' perception of the quality of the candidates and the difficulty of the papers. In other words, these boundaries are not uniformly applicable from one year to the next.

The amount of time allowed for the examination is 1 hour and 30 minutes. It is therefore advised that you spend 10 minutes reading through each part of the questions and sketching out a plan for each section. In this way you will have approximately the same time in minutes per question as there are marks allocated, although you would do well to go quickly on the 4- and 8-mark questions to allow yourself time to check through your whole paper at the end.

## Assessment objectives

There are four assessment objectives, or sets of skills, in each unit of AS and A-level economics. When questions are set, these skills are very much in the mind of the examiners. The objectives are **knowledge**, **application**, **analysis** and **evaluation**.

These are defined in the following table. In the overall assessment of the A-level, the four assessment objectives count equally. However, there is a greater weighting given to the first two objectives in AS, and a greater weighting to the final two objectives in A2.

| Objective | Assessment objectives |
|-----------|----------------------|
| 1 | **Knowledge and understanding:** identify the relevant economic points as outlined in the specified content. |
| 2 | **Application:** use the data provided and other real-world data to apply economic knowledge and critical understanding to problems and issues. |
| 3 | **Analysis:** breakdown economic problems and issues, using economic methodology. |
| 4 | **Evaluation:** weigh up economic arguments and evidence, making informed judgements and justified conclusions. |

### Knowledge and understanding

This objective involves the ability to define key terms and to demonstrate an understanding of economic models relevant to the unit in question. In Unit 2 you are expected to be able to define terms such as inflation, productivity, supply-side policies and purchasing power parities (PPPs).

### Application

The objective here is to show that you can apply macroeconomic theory to real-world data presented in the data-response questions. Anecdotal evidence may be used, such as a reference to events that you have read about recently. The latest movements in the main Bank of England interest rate might be relevant, for example, or the strength of the pound against other major currencies. The examination is a data-response paper rather than an essay paper, so you will need to refer to the data in order to earn full marks in this skill area.

### Analysis

This assessment objective requires some economic theory to be used, in a logical way, to break down an argument. Often the best way of answering such questions is to use transmission mechanisms, which are logical economic stepping stones in your argument. For example, rather than just saying that a fall in interest rates might raise the level of aggregate demand, you could add a step saying that a fall in interest rates encourages people to take out more loans, and therefore consumer spending increases, which is likely to increase aggregate demand. If you then go on to describe the multiplier effect, you will receive high analysis marks.

### Evaluation

The key here is to demonstrate critical distance from the issues being discussed. The mini-essay and two other sections of each question will require some evaluation, and this is indicated by command words such as 'to what extent', 'examine', 'discuss' and 'assess'. Of the 80 marks available for Unit 2, 20 are allocated to this skill, 12 of which are reserved for the mini-essay. Use signposts to mark out the evaluation element to help examiners to distinguish clearly between your script and those of others with words such as 'however' and 'it depends'.

Methods for gaining evaluation marks include contrasting *short-term* with *long-run* effects, discussing the *for* and the *against* of an argument, criticising any *bias* presented in the data, drawing out the *wider context* of the discussion, and coming to a *reasoned conclusion*.

## Grade boundaries

Performance descriptions have been set for the A/B and E/U boundaries by all A-level examining boards. These are split up into the four assessment objectives. The official Edexcel descriptions are reproduced below, with the author's own examples and comments in *italics*.

### Knowledge

| Grade A/B boundary | Grade E/U boundary |
| --- | --- |
| Candidates demonstrate detailed knowledge and understanding of a wide range of content, including terminology, institutions and models. | Candidates can demonstrate some knowledge from the specification including terminology, institutions and models. |

*You do not need to know everything to get an A grade, but you should be able to make precise definitions of key terms such as the wealth effect.*

### Application

| Grade A/B boundary | Grade E/U boundary |
| --- | --- |
| Candidates can apply the relevant toolkit (body of concepts, models, numerical and graphical techniques, theory and terminology) with clarity and incisiveness in familiar and unfamiliar scenarios. | Candidates apply some elements of the relevant economics toolkit in a range of scenarios. |

*You must be able to use the data, and this is a skill that comes with practice. You should remember that the questions are drawn from the data, and it is your job to make that connection clear.*

### Analysis

| Grade A/B boundary | Grade E/U boundary |
| --- | --- |
| Candidates demonstrate, for the most part, ability to explain logically complex economic problems, models, theories and techniques. | Candidates demonstrate some ability to explain complex economic problems, models, theories and techniques, or more familiarity with economics problems and issues that are less complex. |

*This skill involves being able to break down an argument in a logical way. For example, working through the primary product market diagram is a basic skill, but understanding the declining terms of trade argument is more complex.*

### Evaluation

| Grade A/B boundary | Grade E/U boundary |
|---|---|
| Candidates evaluate effectively straightforward economic arguments and evidence, for example by: prioritisation; making reasoned judgements; presenting well-supported conclusions. | Candidates demonstrate some ability to evaluate straightforward economic arguments and evidence. |

*Examiners in general enjoy marking scripts that are 'clear cut' rather than 'middle of the road'. The easiest way to place your script above the rest is to evaluate. Evaluation is not just about having an opinion or making an unsupported judgement. It is about justifying your arguments, developing your reasoning, seeing the value of alternative viewpoints and prioritising the options you have presented.*

Even if you get parts of your answer wrong, you can still gain an A grade. Examiners apply *positive marking*, which means that what is of value will be accepted, but what is wrong will be ignored. Candidates often cross out a perfectly good piece of analysis. Leave the crossing out to the examiner — you might just earn some marks even if it isn't the best you can say.

## Planning your revision: general points

Start on the first Monday of the first clear week of the Easter vacation. Don't allow yourself to think of this as a holiday. The summer break will be much more fun if you use this one as a crammer. If you cannot trust yourself to be at a desk by Monday morning, book yourself into a revision course or fix a session at the local library for free internet access. You have to be disciplined in your revision; otherwise you are wasting your time.

Educationalists agree that short, sharp bursts of revision are the most effective — after an hour or even 45 minutes your mind wanders. You must be comfortable and unstressed when you revise, although an adrenalin rush or a deadline may help you focus. Give yourself a carrot-and-stick motivation method: incentives as well as punishments. For example, going shopping — if that's your thing — should be a reward for a certain number of hours' work, or not being able to watch your favourite soap might be a suitable punishment if you have not clocked up the hours.

Break up your revision time. Don't think that by staring at books the information will magically be absorbed and that you will be able to regurgitate it. Use sticky notes or revision cards, get friends and family to test you, write some 'night-before notes' for last-minute cramming, and use the internet — as long as you don't allow it to become a distraction.

There are plenty of interactive websites where you can test yourself as you go along. The main problem with internet revision is finding reliable and relevant material. You can waste time by looking at the wrong sites, wrong levels or wrong subject areas. There are many sites designed specifically for you. Go to the Edexcel website at **www.edexcel.org.uk** and use the internal search engine to find the 'Getting Started' guide. Several websites are recommended, as well as further reading.

If you find yourself getting bored, stop and change tack. When you are interested in an issue, this will come across in your answers. Examiners reward lively and well-argued responses and anything that is learnt by rote is easily spotted. If you're bored, think how the examiner must feel.

When starting revision it is easy to get disheartened — for example, to get bogged down in the detail, or to think that you know very little about macroeconomics and give up. You should survey the material for the entire unit well before you sit down to do your final revision. At this time you should:

- **Check that you have covered all elements of the specification.** The specification can be downloaded from the Edexcel website at the above address. The 'GCE from 2008' details all the areas that can be questioned. The code for the paper is 8EC01.
- **Get your notes and past papers in order.** Use the specification as the 'contents' page for each section of your notes — you could use the topic sections in this guide as the basis for your file sections. You could print out the specification, then tick or highlight each block as you progress. Check that you have notes for each section and at least one example question on each topic. On Google, type 'free papers Edexcel economics' and you will find at least 4 years' worth, with mark schemes. You will need to know your 5-digit centre number. Select 'Business and Economics', then 'Economics'. If you are in any doubt about which section your notes should be filed under, ask your teacher for help.
- **Download the Sample Assessment Materials and the Getting Started brochure from the Edexcel website.** (**www.edexcel.com/gce2008/business/ economics/8EC01/Pages/as.aspx**). The Sample Assessment Materials provide practice papers with fully explained mark schemes. The Getting Started brochure (listed on the website as 'Tutor Support Materials') is a set of hints for teachers and gives you some idea of the direction you might pursue if you missed a lesson.
- **Make sure that your figures are up to date.** You will not have to remember specific figures about the macroeconomy, but it would help if you had a good impression or overview of the UK economy. For example, you should know whether there is a current account deficit, whether inflation is within target, and whether unemployment is rising or falling. This kind of 'at a glance' information can be found quickly on the UK snapshot pages at **www.statistics.gov.uk/glance**
- **Make sure that you cover every topic, even if you specialise in chosen areas.** The questions in Unit 2 tend to cover large sections of the specification, and although you choose one from two questions, there will not be many areas you can avoid.
- **Form a mental picture.** Under time pressure and in a hot exam hall where there is a lot of shuffling and paper turning, it is easy to find that your mind blanks out.

It is useful in these moments to be able to picture a page of your notes in your mind, and work from there. This means that during preparation you need an orderly system, and you must be very clear in your layout. Recall is also easier if you revise in the same conditions in which you will be writing the exam paper. So switch off the music, the iPhone or e-mails that arrive on your screen.

- **Make use of your friends and family.** Arguments are not always a bad thing. By disputing the issues you will see both sides of a question, and by defending yourself you will develop all the skills needed for evaluation.

- **Time yourself.** Ask your teachers if you can submit some of your homework as timed pieces. But make sure that you get your notes clearly sorted before you set the clock — don't just write off the top of your head. There are practice questions in this book; you can find others on the Edexcel website and in current journals such as *Economics Today*. Many students find this the best way to gain confidence in exam preparation.

- **Be informed.** You need a daily dose of current affairs: quality newspaper articles and online or TV/radio news items are often concerned with economic issues. Anecdotal evidence — examples from the world around you — is also helpful for application of the subject content. For example, you may notice that exchange rates are falling in countries which are cutting their interest rates. Ask yourself why this is. Important conclusions can be drawn from these simple observations.

### A 4-week structured revision plan

|  | Week 1 | Week 2 | Week 3 | Week 4 |
|---|---|---|---|---|
| **Day 1** | Measurements: economic growth | Human Development Index | Aggregate demand | Macroeconomic policy objectives |
| **Day 2** | Measurements: inflation | Other measures of growth and development | Aggregate supply | Demand-side policies |
| **Day 3** | Measurements: employment and unemployment | Income and wealth | Equilibrium real output | Supply-side policies |
| **Day 4** | Measurements: current account of the balance of payments | Economic growth – causes, constraints and costs | The multiplier | Macroeconomic policy conflicts |
| **Day 5** | Exam practice: do the first data-response question from this guide | Exam practice: do the second data-response question from this guide | Exam practice: do the third data-response question from this guide | Exam practice: do the fourth data-response question from this guide |

For final revision in the weeks leading up to the examination, you could write summaries of your notes — short versions of a theoretical process will help you to be sure of the basics, from which you can build your arguments in the exam. Half an hour a day for a fortnight has much greater value than a day of solid revision — and it might also be more interesting. Your mind plays with the ideas when you are not sitting at your desk, and you will realise that there are gaps in your understanding that you can address when you go back to your notes the next day.

## How to answer the questions

The data-response questions for Unit 2 tend to come from newspaper and online articles. It is therefore well worthwhile getting into the habit of reading a broadsheet newspaper such as the *Financial Times, Guardian, Times* or *Independent*, or watching the news reports that are filed on the BBC and FT.com websites. *The Economist* has good articles which you can listen to on the way to school or college if you download them on to your iPod. Listen to Radio 4 before 9 a.m. or BBC2's *Newsnight* at 10.30 p.m., and ask yourself whether the features would make good Unit 2 questions. Question the journalism, don't just accept it. Give reasons why there might be bias. It is eye opening to read about the same event in different journals, or to watch it on different news channels. Try to detach yourself from the viewpoint of the journalist and offer an opposing view.

You should be up to date in your knowledge of the main trends in the economy at the time of the examination and for the previous 5 years or so. A good way to do this is to look at summary websites such as the main page on **www.statistics.gov.uk** or the education section at **www.bankofengland.co.uk**. There are websites designed specifically for schools such as **www.tutor2u.net/blog/index.php/economics** and **www.economics4u.co.uk**, all of which are built by teachers who currently teach A-level Economics. You will find further resources there, which are continually updated.

In the Unit 2 papers, the essay sections and *two* other parts of both questions 1 and 2 are evaluative, beginning with key words such as 'examine', 'assess', 'to what extent' and 'discuss'. It is therefore vital that you adopt a critical approach, as marks will be reserved for this. Avoid the temptation of reeling off all you know about a subject without structuring your answer to the actual question set. Be sure to come to an evaluative conclusion at the end.

Here are some more tips:
- **Choose your question carefully.** You have 5 minutes to read through the questions. Although you might see some others in the exam hall starting in the first minute or so, you might also see them crossing through whole pages when they realise they have started the wrong question for them. It is better to be able to make a reasonable attempt at *all* the parts of a question than to answer a question where you might be really confident on one part but have to bluff your way on another. Remember, examiners are trained to spot waffle. In addition, candidates get very enthusiastic when they see a question that they have attempted before, but this often leads to a surprisingly bad performance. If the question is worded slightly differently, whole chunks of the answer might get marked as 'not relevant'.

- **Think through your answer — sketch out a plan if this helps you.** If you do provide a plan, it makes it easy for the examiner to see your focus; and if you run out of time, there might even be some marks for the plan. Don't cross it out.
- **Look very carefully at the demands of the question.** If you are asked to give *consequences* or effects, don't waste your time starting out with *causes*. If the question is about development indicators, you must not confine your discussion to measurements of economic growth.
- **Be very strict with your time allocation for each question.** There are 80 marks, and 80 minutes if you have given yourself 10 minutes to read the questions.
- **Try to avoid using asterisks and continuations at the end of your answer.** Although the examiner will, of course, read such additions, the train of thought may be lost if your answer is disjointed and the examiner has to search to find the rest of your answer.
- **Use the economic terms precisely.** Define the key terms in the question, and continually return to the question to ensure that your answer is relevant. This is particularly important on questions involving statistical tools, such as 'base year' and 'income distribution'.
- **Use 'signposts'.** It may be very clear to *you* where your argument is going, and writing 'first', 'secondly', 'thirdly', etc. might feel clumsy. But this kind of signposting gives your writing a structure, and makes it easier for the examiner to concentrate on content and not get lost in your style. It is also worth making it very clear to the examiner where you have attempted to gain evaluation marks. You can do this by starting a sentence or paragraph with such words or phrases as 'however', 'on the other hand', 'in the long run' and 'it depends'.
- **Come to a *reasoned* conclusion.** Ideally, each intermediate paragraph should contain an intermediate conclusion. This should be a summing up of the stage that you have reached in your argument, building up to an overall judgement of the issue that the question poses. When you start each paragraph, look again at the question and check that you are still being relevant, and when you reach the conclusion, you could return to the wording of the question with a direct answer. However, do not be too bold in your answer — there is rarely a straight *yes or no* answer. Whatever your conclusion, there are always going to be problems, and these should be stated.
- **Identify the economic theory behind the question.** Questions tend to be set with economic theory in mind. If at all possible, use the relevant theory rather than writing a general answer. Don't hesitate to use theoretical models and economic terms in your answers.
- **Make use of the text or data provided.** This is a data-response paper, not a memory test. While not all the answers will be embedded in the text, you will be able to use the text or other data for each part. If you don't, you will fail to pick up easy marks. However, don't use more than a few words in quotation marks, and remember that the data might be inaccurate, incomplete or biased. If you can comment on the possible unreliability of the data, you will probably earn some evaluation marks.

- **Look carefully at the scale of graphs.** There may be a scale on each side of a chart, which helps you to spot patterns, but these must be used carefully as you identify which data relate to which scale.
- **When the mark base is higher, go deeper.** You cannot be expected to evaluate *every* relevant point, and the opportunity cost of covering every issue is that you cannot attempt to unravel the complex issues. Bullet points are signs of information being learned — assessment objective 1, but little more. You should instead write solid paragraphs which develop each point, and give examples and counter-arguments.
- **Focus.** Address every word in the mini-essay question. Does the question make any assumptions or give a specific context? This will put you on an evaluative footing from the start. Don't be content with simply defining the words in the question: try to highlight a critical issue or theme. Keep your eye on the question throughout your answer. Any irrelevant material will have a line drawn through it, earning zero marks. Think of the opportunity cost.

# Content
# Guidance

This section focuses on the **macroeconomic** concepts and models that students need to understand for Unit 2: Managing the Economy. The information is organised under the following headings:

- Measurements of economic performance
- Income flows and wealth effects
- Aggregate demand and supply
- Economic growth — causes, constraints and costs
- Macroeconomic objectives of governments
- Policy instruments

# Measurements of economic performance

## Economic growth

There are two meanings of the term **economic growth**: **actual growth** is an increase in real incomes or **gross domestic product (GDP)**; and **potential growth** is an increase in the productive capacity in a country.

If economic growth is measured using national income, then the value is meaningless unless the figures are given in real rather than nominal terms. Real values have been adjusted to remove the effects of inflation, whereas nominal values are the current incomes that you would see if they were unadjusted.

Furthermore, for GDP to have any significance in terms of standards of living, figures must be given per head (or 'per capita'). If a country's income increases by 10% but the population increases by 20%, people are actually worse off per head.

Another important distinction required when measuring economic growth is to look at *values* rather than *volumes*. Firms might achieve higher sales figures because they sell more in volume or number of products, but if those sales are worth less per unit then they are not in fact seeing an increase in the value of their output. As an example, consider Germany and China. Germany is the biggest exporter in the world by *value*, whereas China exports much more in terms of *volume* of goods.

### How is GDP measured?

Gross domestic product is the sum of all goods and services produced in a country in 1 year. It is also the sum of all incomes earned in 1 year, and the sum of all expenditure in one country in 1 year. Consider it as a circular flow of income where for everything that is earned, something must be produced and something must be spent. The government measures all three flows: goods, income and expenditure, which in theory should amount to the same figure (currently around £1.4 trillion in the UK). However, in practice, errors and omissions mean that there are some discrepancies.

Increases in GDP are therefore a sign that a country is experiencing increasing incomes, output and spending. On the face of it, this is a good thing because people can have more goods and services, implying that they have a better standard of living. However, there are many reasons why this might not be the case. If I earn more, it may be that I work longer hours and have more work pressures, or that I have a higher cost of living, such as increased mortgage payments. Pollution is likely to increase as I travel more miles, and there are a whole range of social costs that may be incurred.

Standards of living therefore include factors besides economic growth, although few believe that economic growth has no part to play in increasing living standards.

## Problems of comparison

Let's say that economic growth is 10% in China, 6% in Bangladesh and around 2% in the UK (you can see current figures at **www.imf.org/external/datamapper**). These figures may mask several differences not accounted for in GDP statistics:

- **Subsistence, barter and the black economy.** If farmers consume their own output, if goods are traded without the price system (e.g. by barter), or if goods are paid for without being declared for tax purposes, then national income will not reflect the true standard of living.

- **Currency values.** When trying to compare countries, there is a difficulty in knowing whether to use the official value of a currency or the purchasing power of that currency. This is discussed in the section on the Human Development Index, pp. 26–27.

- **Income distribution.** When comparing countries' income per head, some sense of the income distribution should also be taken into account. In some cases, a large proportion of income is earned by a very few, which makes the mean income much higher than the income enjoyed by the ordinary person. In this way, the general standard of living in a country can appear higher than it really is for most people.

- **Size of the public sector.** If much of the spending in the economy is by government, it might or might not improve welfare for the population.

- **Jam today or jam tomorrow?** Spending on investment goods might mean standard of living increases in the future, but at the expense of living standards today. It is better to take account of future growth patterns rather than simply considering today's income, and stark economic growth figures should be broken down to look at the investment element.

- **Quality issues.** Spending on schools might be high, for example, but how can we measure quality? Are improving results enough to prove that living standards are rising?

These problems in comparing GDP figures between countries and over time mean that comparisons of living standards are likely to be inaccurate if they are based solely on GDP. However, real income growth per head is a good guide if these other factors can be taken into account.

### Examination skills and concepts

- The rate of increase in GDP in real terms is the rate of actual economic growth. It means there is more spending, higher incomes and higher output in the economy.
- The rate of increase in productive possibilities is the rate of potential economic growth. There is more capacity in the economy, which might be because the labour supply has increased, there has been investment, or productivity has increased.

### Common examination errors

- Confusing levels of income (GDP) with economic growth (increases in GDP).
- Confusing constant prices (or real) GDP with current (or nominal) GDP.

**Useful exercises**

- There are several websites such as **www.imf.org/external/datamapper** where you can move your mouse around a map of the world and see growth rates or incomes per head. Do you observe that developing countries tend to have higher growth rates than developed ones?

**Links and common themes**

- The issues of the external costs of increased economic growth are discussed in Unit 1. You do not need to know the externalities diagram for Unit 2, but the concept of spillover effects is the same.
- Both an increase in aggregate demand and an increase in aggregate supply may increase the rate of growth in an economy, but not always. (See the section on economic growth, pp. 38–42.)
- Growth can increase living standards, but policies to increase growth might worsen the environment or widen income gaps. (See the section on macroeconomic policy conflicts, pp. 44–47.)
- Growth is a necessary but not sufficient condition to relieve poverty in developing countries. This is a topic you are likely to discuss in Unit 4: The Global Economy.

# Inflation

**Inflation** is a sustained rise in the general price level. The general price level is measured using an index such as the **consumer prices index (CPI)**. The reason for using an index is that percentage changes can be shown easily, and it makes effective comparisons possible.

Two surveys need to be undertaken. One is to collect information about what people buy, currently known as the expenditure and food survey. This involves collecting information from a sample of nearly 7,000 households in the UK using self-reported diaries of all purchases, including food eaten out. The proportion of income spent on each item is used to ascertain weighting. For example, if 10% is spent on food, then 10% of the weighting is assigned to food.

The second survey is of prices. The price survey is undertaken by civil servants who collect data once a month about changes in the price of the 650 most commonly used goods and services in a variety of retail outlets. Because similar items can be bought in high- and low-cost shops, a selection of prices is gathered for each item, with 120,000 prices gathered in all. The price changes are multiplied by the weights to give a price index; you can measure inflation from this by calculating the percentage change in this index over consecutive years.

**Assessing the measure of inflation**

Since December 2003, the UK government's target for CPI inflation has been 2% (±1%). This means that small price rises are acceptable to the UK government. If prices rise by more than 3% they become a concern, but if they begin to rise by less than 1%, or even fall, then risks of deflation and even a recession might arise.

One problem with the CPI measure is that it does not include housing costs such as mortgage interest repayments or rent. Monthly mortgage payments often form a large part of a household's spending and are certainly a cost of living for almost 10 million households in the UK, with an average mortgage debt of £130,000. So if the CPI rises by only 2% and inflation seems to be under control, a rise in interest rates means that many households will nevertheless be experiencing the effect of higher mortgage payments.

For many people, wage increases are linked to the rate of inflation, and if the CPI measure is used, wage increases will fail to take into account a large part of house-hold expenditure in the form of housing costs. A more appropriate measure for wage increases is the **retail price index (RPI)**. This is more inclusive than the CPI, but it is not as reliable for international comparisons and the statistical method of basing the data is also unique to the UK. Moreover, because the RPI includes the cost of mortgage interest repayments and these will rise when interest rates are raised, any interest rate rise implemented to tackle inflation will have a one-off effect of making inflation appear worse, which makes the policy-makers look incompetent.

There are several other problems with the CPI measure:
- CPI measures the cost of living only for an *average* household. The top and bottom 4% income brackets are not included; nor are pensioners.
- There are sampling problems: only 57% of households respond to the survey, and when they do respond they might not give accurate information about recent spending of various members within the household.
- The 650 items in the 'basket' are changed only once a year, but tastes and fashions change more quickly than this. In addition, the basket does not reflect the fact that changes in retail outlets such as 'buy one, get one free' temporarily change people's spending habits.
- For people with atypical spending patterns, such as vegetarians and non-drivers, the CPI will be unrepresentative. For example, those who often buy rail tickets will experience inflation well above 2%.
- When the quality of goods changes, the measure breaks down because it is not comparing like with like. If I bought a more expensive mobile phone this year than last year, the price change might not be the result of inflation but because I wanted an upgrade.

### Examination skills and concepts
- Inflation is a general and sustained increase in prices, measured by a change in a weighted index of prices such as the CPI.
- An index is used to make comparisons over time and between countries. A base year is chosen and given the value 100, and changes are shown as percentage changes relative to the base year.

### Common examination errors
- Confusing price levels (e.g. CPI) with rates of inflation. The rate of inflation may fall even when price levels are still rising. Can you explain this?

- When asked 'how is inflation measured?' many students waste a lot of time by saying what inflation is. The focus of the answer should be on the two types of survey involved, and there is opportunity cost involved in defining terms that are not required by the question.
- Measures that exclude the cost of mortgage interest repayments, such as the CPI, are often wrongly described as 'excluding mortgages'. No measures of inflation include the mortgage itself, because the mortgage debt does not change with inflation. If anything, mortgages decrease in real terms in times of inflation.

**Useful exercises**

- Visit **www.statistics.gov.uk** and calculate your own rate of inflation using the 'personal inflation calculator' (type these words into the site's main search engine). Then imagine you are your granny and do the same. Do you think incomes for students and pensioners should be linked to a measure of inflation more reflective of both of your spending patterns?

## Employment and unemployment

The **level of employment** is the number of people in work, while the **rate of employment** is the proportion of people in work relative to the size of the workforce. The **workforce** consists of those people who are at work or those of working age who are willing and able to work (i.e. the employed *and* the unemployed).

The **unemployed** are people who are willing and available to work, but are not currently employed. The **level of unemployment** is the number out of work, and the **rate of unemployment** gives this figure as a proportion of the workforce.

There are two main ways of measuring unemployment. The International Labour Organisation uses the **Labour Force Survey**, which is now the official measure used in the UK. This involves a face-to-face interview followed by a quarterly telephone survey of 60,000 households, asking several questions including whether anyone in the household has been out of work for 4 weeks and is ready to start in the next 2 weeks. The questions relate to anyone over the age of 16, and it is therefore a more inclusive survey than the claimant count (see below). However, the survey data are 6 weeks out of date by the time they are published, which happens every month.

The **claimant count** is a measure of unemployment which records the number of people who are claiming jobseekers' allowance (JSA). There is some stigma attached to claiming benefits, so not everyone who is eligible to claim does so, and many are not eligible because the criteria for eligibility are very tight. For example, if you have resigned from your previous job within the last 6 months, or have refused three jobs that you have been offered, then you cannot claim.

In order to gain the full benefit of around £60 a week, you need to have made a certain number of National Insurance Contributions by working in the past. You also have to prove, in an interview at the job centre every 2 weeks, that you are looking for work. Under the rules of the New Deal, you might be denied benefits unless you actively involve yourself in training or work placements. After 6 months of claiming JSA you will be means tested, and claims are substantially reduced if you have a partner who earns or if you have savings above £8,000; payments are stopped altogether if you have more than £16,000. You must be over 18 and below retirement age. If you are unable to work, or are working in a voluntary capacity for more than 16 hours a week, you cannot claim.

The claimant count therefore does not present the full picture of unemployment. It is quick and cheap to obtain these data, however, and it is a useful measure of hardship — after all, you are not very likely to claim jobseeker's allowance if you don't need the money between jobs.

### Examination skills and concepts

- The unemployment level in the UK is around 1.6 million according to the Labour Force Survey, and at a 30-year low of 0.8 million according to the Claimant Count measure.
- Having two measures gives a broader picture of the problem of unused resources, but there are clearly some problems with measuring unemployment.
- Employment is just over 29 million, meaning that in the UK almost one in every two people in the population works. The employment rate — the percentage of workers relative to the number who are able and willing to work — is around 75%.

### Common examination errors

- Although many candidates can explain the distinction between the two types of unemployment measure, many cannot explain how one measure can rise while the other falls, or why they might come closer together or move further apart. To do this you need to know the deficiencies of each measure.

### Useful exercises

- Visit www.statistics.gov.uk and in the 'Economy' section search for the questions asked in the Labour Force Survey. Consider reasons why the data that the answers produce might be unreliable.
- One explanation for the relative changes in the Labour Force Survey and the claimant count is the stage of the economic cycle. List two reasons why this might be so and check them with your teacher or the 'Labour market' section of the www.statistics.gov.uk website.
- Look up the JSA on www.jobcentreplus.gov.uk to find out all the eligibility criteria.

### Links and common themes

- When there are unemployed resources such as labour, the economy is operating inside its production possibility frontier (see Unit 1).
- Spare capacity is also a sign that there is an output gap, which is equivalent to the relatively elastic part of the aggregate supply curve, discussed on pp. 34–36.
- Inflation can redistribute incomes (e.g. from savers to borrowers), and some analysts believe that tolerating inflation means that lower levels of unemployment can be enjoyed. However, inflation makes a country less competitive if its inflation rate is

higher than those of its main trading partners. This could mean that a current account deficit develops or that the exchange rate falls, which is even more inflationary. These conflicts and compounding problems are discussed in the section on 'Conflicts between objectives', pp. 44–47.

### Types and costs of unemployment

There are two very different views on unemployment. On one side, in the 'classical view', there are only unemployed people who are not able and willing to work at the going wage rate. In other words, if people would accept a lower wage they could find jobs. In this view all unemployment is therefore just a short-term problem and the best solution is 'laissez faire' — that is, leave the market to get on with it, and eventually the problem of unemployment will go away.

If people accept lower wages then the costs of living will fall as firms do not need to charge such high prices, so in fact workers will find the lower wages are acceptable once they start working. For this reason it is also called 'real wage' unemployment, where wages have been forced above the market-clearing wage. People who believe that this is the only cause of unemployment think that out-of-work benefits should be cut, trade unions should be curtailed and there should not be a minimum wage. Thus, unemployed people will be forced to work.

In the opposing, 'Keynesian' view, people can be unemployed even in the long run. This is because there is insufficient aggregate demand in the economy. If you agree that the economy can be in equilibrium but not everyone has a job then you are arguing that there is **demand deficient** unemployment or **cyclical unemployment**. Keynes said that if people do not spend, and save too much, then there are multiplier effects in the economy, and less spending means there are fewer job opportunities. If people are losing jobs then there will be even less spending and so the vicious circle continues. Even if wages are cut there will not be more people employed — in fact lower wages will mean that there is even less spending, so even fewer people are needed in employment.

Apart from saving too much, other reasons for demand deficient unemployment are lack of business confidence; and increase in the value of a currency; slow rates of productivity growth relative to other countries; external shocks such as oil price rises (oil is imported and demand is price inelastic, so if prices rise there will be less spending in the UK); and increased use of imports from low wage economies.

Another argument for employment problems that are not linked solely to labour being unwilling to work at the going rate is that the economy is undergoing structural change, and therefore different types of labour are required. The skill set of those, for example, who are trained in manufacturing will not have much value in a business based in the service sector. Clearly, over time, as fewer people are being trained for manufacturing and more for services, this kind of **structural unemployment** will disappear. But as Keynes said, 'in the long run we are all dead', so in the view of many there ought to be proactive policies put in place to deal with both demand-deficient and structural kinds of unemployment.

There will always be **frictional unemployment** — that is, people who are moving from one job to another — but this kind of unemployment is a sign of a healthy, flexible labour market with people willing to change jobs in order to improve their prospects.

*Costs of unemployment*

The costs of unemployment to the economy include:

- **The cost to the individual and dependents.** People will have lower incomes and living standards will fall. However there is a wider unseen cost, as people out of work lose morale and their skill sets can become quickly obsolete.
- **The cost to firms.** Firms will find that people spend less, so they will have to lower prices and will make less profit. However, it may mean that people are more willing to stay in their jobs owing to fear of unemployment, so they may be willing to work harder.
- **The cost to government.** As unemployment rises the government has to pay more in jobseekers' benefits and will receive less in tax.

## Current account of the balance of payments

The **balance of payments** is a record of payments between one country and the rest of the world. The most significant element of it for your AS exam is the **current account**, which records trade in goods, trade in services, investment income and transfers. A country such as Germany, which exports a large number of high-value goods, has a **surplus** on the current account, meaning that more money flows in (for the purchase of German goods and services by foreigners) than flows out for imports. On the other hand, a country that enjoys a high living standard and a high level of confidence, and which is not as successful in export markets, is likely to be running a current account **deficit** where outflows are greater than inflows. Examples are the USA, Spain and the UK.

On its own, a balance of payments deficit on current account is not a problem for an economy as long as it can be funded, but it becomes a problem as reserves of foreign currencies begin to run low. It might mean that the currency falls in value, which is inflationary (imports become more expensive). It might be a sign that the country is becoming uncompetitive (costs rising relative to trading partners) and might in the long run mean that a painful readjustment, such as tax increases, is required to stop people overspending.

**Trade in goods** measures the movement of tangible products across international borders. The UK is a large exporter of pharmaceuticals and cars, but a major importer of foodstuffs and, since 2005, a net importer of oil and gas. **Trade in services** measures movement of intangible output. The UK is a major exporter of banking and insurance services, but an importer of foreign holidays (because the British like to go abroad).

**Investment income** is a measure of interest, profit and dividends that are rewards for capital investments in another country. For example, if a British person buys shares in a US company, the shares will not appear on the current account, but any dividends will appear as a positive figure on the UK current account. Finally, **transfers** refer to the movement of funds for which there is no corresponding trade in goods and services. Examples are taxes paid to the EU, payments to British military personnel working in another country, and when economic migrants send some of their incomes back to their families in another country.

## Causes and costs of an imbalance

The **cause** of a current account imbalance may be that a country is spending too much, or that it is not producing anything that potential customers abroad want to buy. It may be because of the stage in the business cycle, which clearly may be different for different countries at different times, or the strength of the currency. For example, if sterling is strong against the dollar, the UK is likely to export less and import more, because the price of UK exports rises relative to other products on the world market, and imports become relatively cheap in the UK. Perhaps the most significant factor in the UK is the loss of competitiveness in the manufacturing sector owing to higher costs of factors of production in the UK relative to the Far East. It takes time for economies to adjust to changing comparative costs, and during the adjustment process the UK is likely to face an ongoing deficit.

The **costs** of a current account imbalance become significant only when the deficit (or surplus) becomes unsustainable. **Sustainability** means that the needs of the present are met without compromising the ability of future generations to meet their own needs. Persistent deficits can make the value of a currency fall, so in some economies the government might try to buy up surplus currency in order to maintain its value. (This does not happen in the UK.) A fall in the value of the currency may restore competitiveness, as it makes imports seem more expensive and exports relatively cheap on international markets. Persistent deficits see net incomes leave the country, which might mean demand in the domestic country is subdued. If you are a worker you might lose your job, but from the perspective of the Monetary Policy Committee of the Bank of England, this might be a welcome development, preventing the onset of inflation.

### Examination skills and concepts

- The balance of payments records international payments between one country and the rest of the world.
- The current account of the balance of payments records transactions that are income for the recipient, rather than investments or loans. There are four elements in the current account: trade in goods, trade in services, investment income and transfer payments.

### Common examination errors

- One of the most prevalent misunderstandings is the analysis of what happens to the current account of the balance of payments when the interest rate rises. This is only partially within the scope of this unit and will be discussed in detail in Unit 4, but it is important not to argue that 'hot money enters the country and this improves the balance' because hot money is not part of the current account. The best argument to pursue in Unit 2 is that when the interest rate rises, the exchange rate usually rises too, so exports will become less competitive and imports more so.

- Many students cannot understand why holidays abroad are an 'import'. The easiest way to decide whether or not something is an import is to look at the direction of the money flows. If money is leaving the country, the trade is an import.

### Useful exercises

- On Google, type in 'UK balance of payments first release' with the current year to see a summary of the current account in recent years, with simple graphs.
- The 'Pink Book' (type 'Pink Book Balance of Payments' into Google) is more up-to-date and very detailed, but perhaps not so easy to interpret.

### Links and common themes

- Many students find the current account the most mystifying of all the measures of economic performance. This is partly because Unit 2 is a holistic study and you need to know the rest of the unit before this part fully makes sense. Furthermore, it is just a partial look at international trade, which will be covered in more depth in Unit 4.

## Measures of development: the Human Development Index

**Economic development** measures the *quality* of growth, rather than merely an increase in incomes. In order to measure the quality of growth we may take into account access to resources, living standards, the ability to make choices and the sustainability of growth. Composite indicators such as the **Human Development Index (HDI)** have been developed by the United Nations to combine the advantages of GDP measures and non-GDP economic and social indicators.

The HDI is a measure of standards of living used since 1990. It comprises three equally weighted elements: one-third health (measured by life expectancy at birth), one-third education (of which one-third is school enrolment ratio and two-thirds is adult literacy), and one-third GDP per head at **purchasing power parity**. This means that the rate of conversion of the local currency into US dollars is such that the same basket of goods and services could be bought in each country.

There are two ways in which you might come across the Human Development Index. One is as a **rank**, where number 1 is the top and then countries get worse as the number rises. The other way is as an **index**, where the number 1 means the best and 0 is the worst. In an examination you are most likely to see the index, and you should know that 1 to 0.8 is considered to be a high level of human development, 0.8 to 0.5 is medium, and below 0.5 is low.

### Assessing the HDI

The HDI is a helpful measure of development because it uses reliable and fairly easy-to-obtain indicators, takes income into account but qualifies income in terms of the cost of living. The figures chosen have been judged to be those that can be recorded with the most consistency.

However, the HDI has some problems: it gives no indication of the distribution of incomes, and an indication of deprivation might make it more useful. For example, the **Human Poverty Index** is an index developed in 1997 which records what people go without rather than what they have. This might be more useful for governments or donors. Life expectancy is easy to measure but it does not give any indication of the quality of life. The literacy measure might be seen as placing too much emphasis on academic knowledge such as reading and writing. Practical knowledge, such as computer literacy, might have a greater impact on livelihoods and quality of life. Years of schooling might be unreliable if it means that students are repeating years because they cannot make progress.

### Examination skills and concepts

- The Human Development Index is a composite measure of economic development, which combines three factors chosen to represent the broad areas of income, health and education.

### Common examination errors

- A common mistake is to confuse ranks (where 1 is the highest, falling to 177, which is currently Sierra Leone) with index numbers (where 1 is perfect and 0 is where humans cannot live).

### Useful exercises

- Visit the United Nations Development Programme website (www.undp.org) to see the latest Human Development Report. The tables in the back of the report give the GDP, HDI and other indicator ranks.
- Choose any country and find its GDP per head ranking at PPP values and its HDI. Subtract the second from the first. If the figure is positive, the country excels in education and health relative to incomes, and vice versa for a negative outcome.
- You can see the results of this exercise in the final column of Table 1 in the UN Human Development Report. The higher the figure, whether positive or negative, the greater the disparity between purely income measures and health and education measures of human development.

### Links and common themes

- The concept of HDI is invaluable for assessing the performance of developing countries, and the knowledge acquired here is intended to prepare you for the work you will cover in Unit 4.

## Other measures of development

There are many other ways to judge the development of a country. Each has its advantages and disadvantages, and a selection of indicators could be chosen to show changes over time or to compare changes in different countries.

One indicator which signifies not just standards of living but potential for development is the measure of **mobile phones per thousand of the population**. Mobile technology allows a catch of fish to be brought into a port where prices are highest, or can be used to develop a cashless trading system in a country where the currency and finance systems are insecure. Mobiles don't rely on a constant supply of electricity and are therefore a strong indication that a country can develop despite problems in infrastructure.

Another very helpful indicator is the **proportion of workers involved in agriculture**. In Asia and sub-Saharan Africa, around two-thirds of the workforce is employed in agriculture. In Latin America the proportion is around 25%, but in developed countries the figure is usually below 2%. The greater the proportion, the less likely it is that the country has high actual or potential growth. The marginal product of labour in agriculture is likely to be very low, and workers are likely to have little income and little access to other forms of work where incomes could rise. However, living in an agricultural environment does provide some protection from international shocks such as global recession, in that the produce can be life sustaining if not always income generating.

**Problems in using other measures of development**

Many measures have data collection problems. Some data, such as disease indicators, are difficult to gain with accuracy because cause of death might not be known or might be concealed for cultural or political reasons.

Another problem is that indicators can overlap, so although a wider use of indicators might give a broader picture, it might also give a very uneven picture. For example, access to safe water and disease indicators are likely to be closely related, increasing the weight of the health measure relative to incomes and education.

### Useful exercises

- Look at the latest Human Development Report at **www.undp.org** and choose a non-GDP-based indicator, such as newspapers bought per thousand. Think of a reason why it might be a good sign of development (in this case, literacy) and a poor indicator (it depends on the type of newspaper).

### Links and common themes

- Other measures of economic development include absolute and relative poverty. These will be studied in Unit 4.

# Income flows and wealth effects

## Income flows

Imagine the economy as a simple model where there are just households and firms. The **households** own all the factors of production — land, labour, capital and enterprise — and the **firms** are the producing units. Money moves from households to firms when they buy goods and services; and money moves back to households as payment for the use of the factors of production in the form of rent, wages, interest and profit. In this very simple model, known as the **circular flow of income**, money circulates from households to firms and back again, and the more that households spend and the more that firms produce, the higher the levels of income. It does not matter which way you look at it, the income and output in an economy should always be the same, and they are measured by **gross domestic product (GDP)**.

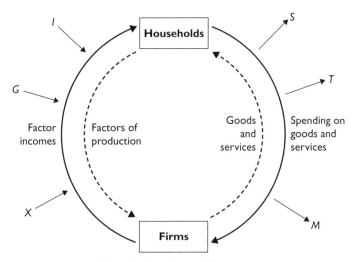

**The circular flow of income**

There are three **leakages** (or withdrawals) from the circular flow of income: savings, tax and imports. If you hide your money under your bed, the economy will slow down a little because there is less money in the circular flow. Similarly, if the government takes money away from the economy in the form of tax and does not spend it, or if people buy more things from abroad than they export, the economy will slow down as money leaves the circular flow. These three leakages effectively determine the size of the multiplier (see below).

By contrast, there are three **injections** into the circular flow. These are investment — which is an increase in the capital stock — government spending and exports. These all increase the circular flow and a change in any of these will be magnified by the multiplier.

The **multiplier** is the number of times a change in incomes exceeds the change in net injections that caused it. It is the knock-on effect on incomes when injections and withdrawals change. For example, if there is a £10 million increase in export values, the inward flow of money to the UK will be re-spent within the UK. When the money is spent it will become other people's incomes. These incomes will be re-spent, and so on.

The importance of the multiplier is that if there is any change in spending in an economy, the final impact on incomes will be much greater than the initial impact. The greater the leakages, the smaller the multiplier. The formula is based on how much of any extra pound earned is re-spent within the economy: that is, **the marginal propensity to consume**. The size of the multiplier in the UK is approximately 1.4, but in developing countries it is often higher, which partly explains their higher growth rates. For example, in a country with a multiplier of 3, a net injection of $10 million will cause a $30 million increase in incomes in total.

If all the injections equal all the leakages, then the economy will be in **equilibrium**; if injections are greater than leakages, the economy will grow; and if leakages are greater than injections, the economy will contract.

## Wealth effects

**Wealth** is the sum of all the assets in an economy. In the UK, most wealth is held in the form of housing (almost 60%); the other major forms of wealth are stocks and shares and capital assets. Wealth is a **stock** concept, whereas income is a **flow** concept — this means that wealth does not have a direct impact on the circular flow of income, but changes in wealth are likely to have an effect on incomes and spending. For example, if you live in a property that increases in value, you might feel more confident about spending in the economy and your increased spending will then become part of the circular flow of income. Moreover, if houses become more expensive, someone could go to their mortgage provider and request mortgage equity release: that is, take out a loan based on the increased wealth. When that loan is spent, the circular flow increases. By contrast, when capital markets take a downturn in the USA, people living on pensions in the UK might find that their incomes fall because dividends on pension funds are often based on capital gains of shares.

### Examination skills and concepts

- Income (e.g. export income) is a flow concept, while wealth (e.g. capital assets) is a stock concept.
- Income is measured by real GDP.
- Wealth in the UK is £6.5 trillion — five times the total income in the economy.
- Most income in the UK is held in the form of housing (59%). The rest is split fairly equally between capital assets and shares.
- Capital assets or stock in the UK amount to £2.6 trillion. This is slightly less than the cost of maintaining all capital stocks in their current condition — a cost known as depreciation.

### Common examination errors

- Thinking that consumption (C) is an injection.
- Arguing that an increase in house prices (wealth) will cause a fall in aggregate demand because 'people don't have as much money to spend on other things'.

### Useful exercises

- The best site for mortgage information is www.bbc.co.uk — on the news page go to Business, then Economy, or watch a recent clip under 'video and audio'. Then you might also visit www.mortgagesmadeeasy.co.uk, www.cml.org.uk (the website of the Council of Mortgage Lenders) or www.mortgageguideuk. co.uk for accessible explanations and arguments about anything to do with mortgages.

# Aggregate demand and supply

'Aggregate' means *added together* — the individual elements that were introduced in microeconomics are totalled in macroeconomics. Aggregate demand and supply analysis brings together the amount that consumers wish to consume and firms wish to produce at any price level. **Aggregate demand (*AD*)** is the total planned expenditure on goods and services produced in the UK. **Aggregate supply (*AS*)** is the total planned output of goods and services. The equilibrium point where they meet determines the average price level and the equilibrium real output level. The price level can be measured by a price index such as the CPI, and the output by real GDP.

The aggregate demand and supply model is probably the most useful tool for macroeconomists, because it gives reasons for changes in the important macroeconomic variables: when price levels increase this is inflation, and when output increases this is economic growth.

## Aggregate demand

Aggregate demand (*AD*) is the total planned expenditure on goods and services produced in the UK. It comprises consumption (*C*), investment (*I*), government spending (*G*) and exports (*X*) minus imports (*M*).

The *AD* curve is downward sloping. This is not because 'people buy more things when they are cheaper' (the most common misunderstanding about the *AD* curve). There are three ways to explain the downward-sloping *AD* curve, any of which is adequate for an answer at AS:

- Lower prices in an economy mean increased international competitiveness, so there are more exports and fewer imports. In other words, net exports are higher at lower prices.
- The total amount of spending will be approximately equal whether prices are high or low because people have approximately the same amount of money to spend, so the area under the curve will be fairly constant. This is known as the **real balance effect**. If you plot a constant area, you will get a **rectangular hyperbola**.
- At higher price levels, interest rates are likely to be raised by the monetary authorities. This means that investment, a component of aggregate demand, will fall and savings might increase.

### The components of aggregate demand and their relative importance
#### Consumption
**Consumption**, or spending by households on goods and services, is the main component of aggregate demand, comprising approximately 65%. It measures the amount that consumers wish to spend at various price levels. One of the key determinants of consumption is the confidence of the consumer, both in terms of job security and in terms of future income prospects. If consumers are feeling confident, they are more likely to make large purchases which they can pay for in the future.

Another determinant is interest rates. Higher interest rates not only leave consumers with less spending money after housing costs, but also increase the cost of hire purchase. A third determinant is the housing market. When house prices accelerate, home owners can extract more equity from their houses, as discussed in the section on 'Wealth effects' (p. 30).

### Investment

There is an inverse relationship between interest rates and the level of investment that firms intend to make. This is because increases in the capital stock have to be financed, and there is an opportunity cost to that finance. Firms often borrow from banks to finance investment, so if interest rates rise, the cost of borrowing rises and firms are less likely to borrow, and therefore less likely to invest. However, investment is not based solely on interest rates, and some argue that the interest elasticity of demand for investment is very low. This is because investors are sometimes driven more by other factors, such as confidence in future sales patterns, what their main competitors are doing, government incentives and regulations, and the prospects for future interest rates than by the current rate of interest.

A change in investment will change the level of aggregate demand, but a change in aggregate demand will also change the level of investment. This circular relationship can be analysed using the **accelerator**, and although this is not required knowledge for the AS examination, it is a useful way of evaluating the role of investment.

### Government spending

Government spending in the UK comprises almost 40% of all spending in the economy, totalling about £590 billion. Government spending need not equal tax revenue and the difference between them is known as a **budget (or fiscal) deficit or surplus**. The government can deliberately manipulate aggregate demand by overspending (running a budget deficit) when there is a slowdown in the economy, and vice versa in a boom. Taxing more heavily in times of abundance is a useful way to put the brakes on the economy, although sometimes governments miscalculate the start of the downturn and cut taxes too early (as in the late 1980s). Similarly, net spending can be increased in a recession, which will reverse the effects of demand deficiency.

Another factor to consider is the **national debt** — the accumulation of budget deficits over the years. The budget needs to balance over the course of the economic cycle, otherwise the government will accrue national debt. Interest payments have to be made on this, and if the government continues to overspend there will be a cost for future generations. In the short run, however, there is some flexibility with the balance of the government's accounts.

### Assessing the impact of an imbalance in the flow of government income

The Keynesian view is that fiscal policy — that is, the deliberate manipulation of government spending and taxation in order to change aggregate demand — is a powerful tool in shifting aggregate demand, made much more effective by the working of the multiplier. In contrast, the classical economists' view is that overspending by the government has a similar effect to printing more money — it is purely inflationary.

There is now some consensus that deliberate fiscal manipulation has a short-run impact, but only if wage demands and other cost pressures are kept in check. There is also much consensus that it is only really through supply-side policies that long-term improvements in equilibrium employment will be achieved, as the *AS* curve shifts to the right (see 'Shifts in the aggregate supply curve', pp. 35–36). But as Keynes would say, 'in the long run we are all dead': that is, by the time the unemployed become employable, they will be past employment age.

### Net exports

Exports represent an injection into the circular flow of income, in that the money paid for goods and services sold abroad enters the domestic flow of income. Imports mean that there is an outflow of money, and exports minus imports gives the total movement of funds, known as **net exports**. (If the value of imports is greater than the value of exports, this will be a negative figure, as in the UK.) There are several reasons why the value of net exports might change.

First, consider a change in the exchange rate. If the exchange rate increases in value against other currencies, imports become cheaper and exports more expensive on world markets. Over time, people respond to these relative price movements and the demand for exports falls and the demand for imports rises. A stronger currency will worsen net exports, whereas a weaker currency will improve the figure.

However, in the short run the price elasticity of demand for exports and imports tends to be low. This may be because contracts have been signed for specific deals in international trade, or because the traded components are a very small percentage of firms' overall costs. For example, an Italian importer of BMW Minis will agree a price in advance of delivery from the UK. If the pound gets stronger against the euro, the price of the cars will remain as per contract. Price elasticity of demand may also be low because of a lack of available substitutes, as in the case of oil. Owing to the low price elasticity of demand for exports and imports, the initial impact of a change in the exchange rate may be the opposite of the one described above.

A second major cause of changes in the value of net exports is changes in the global economy. For example, if there is a recession in the USA, but the UK does not suffer a slowdown, the USA will buy fewer exports from the UK, and will be attempting to export more. Similarly, if there is inflation in the UK, but not in other countries, net exports from the UK will worsen as UK goods become increasingly uncompetitive. A collapse in a stock market in another part of the world may also have direct effects on UK exports via wealth effects.

Thirdly, non-price factors, such as quality and after-sales service, are major determinants of net exports. Germany, for example, cannot compete effectively on price, but the value of its exports exceeds that of any other country owing to its high quality of design and manufacture.

In summary, when any of the components *C*, *I*, *G* or *X* rises, the *AD* curve shifts to the right (see the diagram overleaf). The same happens if imports fall. As a useful evaluation point, it is wise to consider that the above analysis involves changes in *levels* rather than *rates*. In the UK these components do not usually fall, but they may rise more slowly during an economic slowdown, which means that the *AD* curve will still shift to the right, but by increasingly smaller amounts.

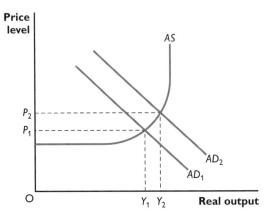

*Effect of a shift in aggregate demand on price and real output*

## Aggregate supply

Aggregate supply is the amount that firms are willing to produce at various price levels. It is largely influenced by productivity, which in turn is influenced by factors such as the costs of production, the level of investment, the availability and efficiency of factors of production and supply-side policies.

There are two views of aggregate supply. The classical view is that in the long run an economy will operate at full capacity and there will be no unemployed resources in the economy: that is, the *AS* curve is vertical. If there are any unemployed resources, the prices of these factors will fall until the surplus disappears.

By contrast, the Keynesian view is that the equilibrium level of output can occur below the full employment level of output. According to this view, the *AS* curve has a backward-bending L shape, with three distinct sections: spare capacity, bottlenecks and full employment. The assumption behind this analysis is that an economy can be at equilibrium when it is not at full employment. In other words, demand deficiency may mean that unemployed resources such as labour will not find work if the economy is left to its own devices.

In section A of the next diagram there is spare capacity. The economy can increase output without any cost pressures. This is because there are unused resources, such as factories not working at full capacity, or unemployed labour. In this section, aggregate demand might shift to the right — for example, through fiscal policy — and equilibrium real output would increase without causing an increase in the price level. The situation is comparable to that of Japan over the past two decades, where there is a lot of scope for increased production, but unemployment persists in the long run.

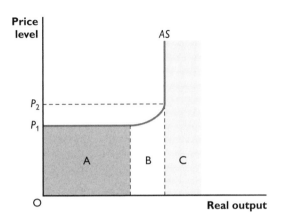

*The Keynesian aggregate supply curve*

Section B in the diagram is the bottlenecks section, where some constrictions in the supply chain cause cost and wage pressures to build up in some areas of the economy. This usually involves a certain type of labour which when in short supply can have its price bid upwards. An example concerns the shortage of construction workers associated with the 2012 Olympics. If aggregate demand expands in this section of the graph, then while the economy will still grow, there will be some inflation.

Section C illustrates full capacity in the economy. All viable workers have work, so if a firm wants to take on more workers it will have to entice them away from other jobs by offering higher wages. In this section of the diagram, if aggregate demand increases, although in the short run there might be some extra spending, the long-term effect will be increased inflation and no increased output.

According to the classical view, section C is the only part of the *AS* curve that occurs. The economy cannot be in equilibrium while there is unemployment. So, if unemployment does exist, it can only result from a short-run failure of the market or from mismanagement by the government.

## Shifts in the aggregate supply curve

Shifts in aggregate supply occur when factors change which will affect most firms. Such factors might relate specifically to the cost of workers (labour market) or the way in which firms compete (product market). Let's consider how changes in both markets might produce a rightward shift of the *AS* curve.

### *Labour market*

In the labour market, a rightward shift in the aggregate supply curve could occur in the following ways:

- **Productivity gap closes.** Productivity is output per unit of input, and if it increases relative to a country's main trading partners then the productivity gap is said to be closing. For example, the gap is currently closing between the UK and France, so while the UK has lower productivity than France, its productivity is increasing over time, which means that costs of production are becoming relatively less expensive in the UK compared to France. However, the gap is widening between the UK and the remainder of its major trading partners.

- **Education and skills improve.** Increased spending on education and training should mean that a country's workforce can produce more output per worker. Education increases the value of the potential output. However, not all education achieves this end. It is not clear that a BA in Madonna Studies or a BSc in Surf Science has a major impact on costs of production in the UK.
- **Health spending increases.** An increase in resources in the health sector should mean that workers have fewer days off sick and are active for longer — often beyond traditional retirement ages. However, spending on health might be absorbed into wage increases for staff in the health service, which would have little overall effect on the level of healthcare. Similarly, the majority of healthcare spending goes on the elderly or very young, neither of which are economically active.

### Product market

In the product market, a rightward (or downward) shift in the aggregate supply curve could occur in the following ways:

- **Sources of raw materials change.** In a developed country like the UK most raw materials are imported, and if global competition increases, UK costs will fall. The cost of these imports depends on demand pressures from other parts of the world as well as supply. If there is a global increase in demand for oil, for example, this will cause the costs of production to increase in the UK because oil is a major production cost in almost all UK firms.
- **Exchange rates fall.** If the euro fell in value relative to the pound, many costs would fall in the UK, meaning that aggregate supply in the UK increases.
- **International trade increases.** As a country opens up to more trade, competition drives down prices and inefficient domestic firms give way to overseas firms with a comparative advantage. So as globalisation develops, aggregate supply increases.
- **Technological advances.** Innovation and investment in new ideas tend to reduce costs for all firms. For example, widespread access to the internet increases competition among firms and also means that firms can be more streamlined. Buying a book, for instance, is now much cheaper online because there are fewer expensive retail outlets to maintain.
- **Regulation changes.** There are many regulations in the UK economy which have been imposed to try to maintain a disciplined economy, for example in the postal and telecommunications services. However, such industries have been increasingly deregulated over the past two decades to increase competition, which in turn imposes its own form of discipline. The net effect is that parcel postage and phone services — costs faced by all firms — have reduced in real terms, shifting aggregate supply to the right (or down).

### Examination skills and concepts

- Aggregate demand is the total amount that is planned to be spent in an economy at any price level.
- Aggregate supply is the output that all firms are willing to supply at any price level.
- Equilibrium real output and price level occur where aggregate demand meets aggregate supply.
- The components of aggregate demand are $C + I + G + (X - M)$ and a change in any one of these will shift the $AD$ curve, with multiplier effects. If aggregate demand increases, the price level is likely to rise and output may rise, depending on the price elasticity of the aggregate supply curve.
- Increases in aggregate supply will tend to lower prices or curb rises in prices. Real output is likely to increase, although this depends on the elasticities where the $AD$ and $AS$ curves cross.

### Common examination errors

- Many students get very confused when drawing $AD/AS$ diagrams, either using micro-economic labels ($D$ and $S$) or shifting $AD$ and $AS$ in the wrong directions. It is best to use simple versions of the diagrams that you understand.
- Unit 2 follows immediately after Unit 1 in the summer slot, so if you are taking the two exams together you need to shake off all notions of microeconomic analysis. Some students ask the invigilator if they can take a comfort break between the two papers — a good opportunity to freshen up and think about aggregates.
- Many $AD/AS$ diagrams are drawn in exams — and indeed in some textbooks — with inflation rather than the price level on the vertical axis. Use the price level label.

### Useful exercises

- On **www.economics4u.co.uk** you can download a pack of materials to guide you through $AD$ and $AS$ shifts from scratch. There is also a set of possible answers in the teachers' section.
- You will certainly be required to draw $AD/AS$ diagrams in your exam, so you might like to sketch all the possible permutations and put them on separate cards. Then rank them in order for the way in which you would use them to solve various macroeconomic problems.

### Links and common themes

- The relationship between exchange rates and net exports can most clearly be understood using the Marshall–Lerner condition and the $J$ curve. This will be explained in Unit 4.
- Fiscal policy is discussed further on pp. 47–48 of this guide, and developed more fully in Unit 4.

# Economic growth — causes, constraints and costs

**Actual growth** can be defined as an *increase in real GDP* and **potential growth** as an *increase in capacity* in the economy. Measures of real GDP tend to fluctuate over the course of an economic cycle. During a **boom**, real GDP rises fast. In a **recession**, it falls for at least two consecutive quarters. During a **slowdown**, the level of GDP may be rising, but rising below the trend.

The difference between *actual output* and either the *trend* or *potential output* is called the **output gap**. The second of these two ways of defining the output gap is shown in the diagram.

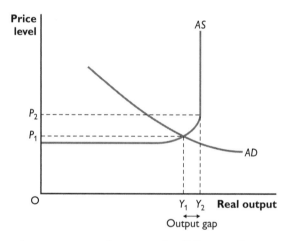

*The output gap shown as the difference between actual output and potential output*

If the economy is growing faster than the trend, pressures will grow in the economy, such as tight labour markets, wage pressures and shortages of raw materials. This is referred to as a **positive output gap**. It may be a sign that the economy is overheating and the inflationary pressures might persuade the Bank of England's Monetary Policy Committee to raise interest rates. However, if the economy is growing below trend, there is likely to be spare capacity in the economy. This situation is known as a **negative output gap**. It means that there is scope for a cut in interest rates, which is less likely to cause inflationary pressures.

## Causes of *actual* economic growth

Economic growth can occur because there is an increase in one of the components in **aggregate demand**, where $AD = C + I + G + (X - M)$.

Here are some examples. Increased consumption might occur because of increased consumer confidence or the availability of credit. Increased investment increases the level of growth, and is itself dependent on the level of growth (i.e. it has an **accelerating** effect on growth rates). Government spending on education or health might cause growth. Export-led growth has the added advantage of improving the current account of the balance of payments.

Growth can also occur because of an increase in **aggregate supply**. This might happen because costs of production fall — for example, labour markets might become more competitive thanks to immigration or an increase in the birth rate — or because of government supply-side policy such as **deregulation** in the markets (removing constraints that limit competition). This is discussed in the section on 'Policy instruments', pp. 47–51.

A shift of the *AD* or *AS* curve to the right should cause an increase in actual growth. However, if aggregate demand increases and the *AD* curve is crossing the vertical part of the *AS* curve, the only effect will be increased prices, not increased GDP. Similarly, if aggregate supply increases and the *AD* curve is crossing the *AS* curve on its horizontal part, there will be no change in the equilibrium and there will be no change in price levels or output.

## Causes of *potential* economic growth

Potential economic growth can only occur when the vertical part of the *AS* curve shifts to the right, increasing the amount that the economy could produce. Using another model, potential economic growth increases when the production possibility curve shifts to the right. Possible causes of the *AS* shift are described in the previous section as well as later in this guide in the section on 'Policy instruments', pp. 47–51.

## Constraints on growth

There are several factors constraining growth:

- **Absence of capital markets.** One of the main reasons why Latin America grows more slowly than the Asian subcontinent is that Asia has more credible and efficient capital markets. In many economies in sub-Saharan Africa, the interest charged on credit, if credit is available at all, is typically over 50%. One of the issues is the **asymmetric information** in credit markets, where the lender knows very little about the borrower and charges higher rates to cover the enormous risk. The only people able to afford these high rates are likely to be among the more corrupt borrowers, which makes it even less likely that people will lend. The market then becomes a **missing market**, in the sense that there is no equilibrium price of credit where buyers and sellers can agree a rate of interest.
- **Government instability.** Where governments are incompetent, or lack transparency or strong political backing, the economy cannot attract inward investment and the currency might be unstable. The government might have a fiscal deficit which means that it has little power to spend money to encourage growth.

This is more extreme if there is political tension, wars or diversion of funds to increase a country's defence.

- **Labour market problems.** A shortage of skilled labour is a major constraint on growth. As countries get richer, birth rates tend to fall dramatically; in the long run this means that the labour supply will fall. One of the most effective policies for reducing this in high-income countries is to allow increased immigration, although in low-income countries the exit of skilled workers (known as the 'brain drain') exacerbates the skill problems.
- **External constraints.** Trade is a key driver of growth. Uneven access to world markets owing to tariffs and subsidies can prevent a country from growing. Global recession or fears of terrorism also slow down trade, as does volatility in exchange rate markets. Figures suggest that for every 3% growth in world trade there is a 1% increase in world GDP, and therefore anything that holds back international trade is likely to act as a constraint on growth.

## Benefits of growth

Growth benefits employees, firms and governments in the following ways:

- **Employees.** Incomes and wealth rise when there is economic growth. Standards of living rise as long as the costs of living do not increase at the same rate. In other words, *real* growth means that *real* incomes rise. Increases in growth can mean that wealth in the form of assets such as shares and houses increases.
- **Firms.** Firms tend to make more profit when there is economic growth. In times of growth, consumer spending usually rises, which means that firms sell more. As revenues and profits rise, firms can take on more workers and are more likely to invest. This increases future growth prospects.
- **Governments.** When incomes and assets rise in price, people pay more income and capital gains tax. Governments also have fewer demands to pay unemployment benefits. So in times of economic growth the government is likely to enjoy a healthier fiscal position.

## Costs of growth

Despite the benefits listed above, growth incurs the following costs:

- **Income inequality.** The unwaged and unskilled are less likely to benefit from increased incomes. While money might eventually 'trickle down' to lower-income groups, there might equally be a two-speed economy where the incomes of some people accelerate but others cannot get out of a low-skill slow lane. The type of production tends to change during periods of economic growth, so there is likely to be short-term unemployment for people who do not have labour market flexibility.
- **Environmental problems.** Depletion of natural resources and external costs such as carbon emissions and other forms of pollution are likely to increase with economic growth. However, high-income governments can use their increased tax revenue to clean up the environment.
- **Balance of payments problems on the current account.** With higher incomes, domestic consumers suck in more imports and there is less incentive

for firms to export. However, if growth were export-led, the current account would improve.

- **Bottlenecks in the economy.** When there is little spare capacity in the economy, factors of production such as skilled labour and fuel rise in price. Monopoly power might also develop, which can be used as a barrier to the entry of new firms (see Unit 3). This can be shown using an increasingly inelastic *AS* curve.
- **Social dislocation and stress.** Higher incomes have to be earned. With increased pay there are usually increased responsibilities. There may be more travel and the need to move further afield as firms grow. However, with higher incomes people can also afford to work fewer hours, go on more luxurious holidays, pay for their children's education or retire early. So social life may or may not improve as the economy grows.
- **Problems of rapid growth.** Rapid growth can cause short-term spikes in prices. If a country grows too quickly there might be bad planning, corner cutting and shoddy workmanship. However, rapid growth might just need time to settle down in terms of income distribution, and a strong government such as that in China can ensure that growth is planned effectively.

### Examination skills and concepts

- Economic growth can be explained in terms of increases in actual GDP or increases in potential GDP.
- When aggregate demand increases, actual GDP will increase, as long as the *AS* curve is not vertical.
- When aggregate supply increases, actual GDP will increase, as long as the *AD* curve does not cross the *AS* curve on a horizontal part of the curve.
- Only a shift of the *AS* curve to the right will cause an increase in potential economic growth.
- The benefits and costs of growth are not easy to measure, and change over time. It is therefore difficult, but important, to assess whether the benefits outweigh costs.
- As growth rates rise, it is likely that the increasing marginal costs will be outweighed by decreasing marginal costs.

### Common examination errors

- Many answers say that 'if there is increased growth there will be inflation'. This is not true if the increase is in potential growth, and not necessarily true if the increase is in actual growth. It depends on the availability of spare resources.

### Useful exercises

- Figures for the output gap in OECD countries are published by the OECD every year. In these figures, a positive output gap is a boom and a negative output gap is a slump. The UK and Germany had slumps in 1990–92. Name another country for which this is true.
- Read an account of London in the winter of 1947, where smog brought the capital to a standstill. To what extent can economic growth be used to explain problems of smog and the cleanliness of much of London in recent years?

- Asymmetric information (in capital markets) has been introduced in Unit 1 and is useful for explaining limits to growth.
- To understand more about asymmetric information in the credit market, read George Akerlof's short article on lemons in 'An economic theorist's book of tales', obtainable cheaply on the internet.
- Constraints on growth in developing countries will be discussed fully when considering limits to growth and development in Unit 4.

# Macroeconomic objectives of governments

There are six main objectives that governments generally wish to pursue:
- increased economic growth (rises in real GDP)
- control of inflation
- reduction in unemployment
- restoration of equilibrium in the balance of payments on current account
- a more equal distribution of income
- protection of the environment

The order of priority varies according to the politics of a particular government and institutional arrangements such as the Monetary Policy Committee. Some governments see the control of inflation as the most important macroeconomic goal. Others, such as governments with a socialist leaning, would focus on the redistribution of incomes and the reduction of unemployment.

## Trends in macroeconomic measures

In the years since the last UK recession of 1990–92, the UK has seen economic growth at a trend of between 2 and 3% per annum, and inflation hardly reaching 3%, although cost pressures from increasing commodity prices threaten to force inflation over the 3% ceiling at the time of writing.

Unemployment, as measured by the Labour Force Survey, has settled at just over 1.6 million (5%) in recent years, with the claimant count at a low of 0.8 million.

The trade in goods of the balance of payments is currently recording a £46 billion deficit, just over 5% of GDP, while the current account deficit as a whole is £46 billion (3% of GDP). The deficit is wider during periods of higher economic growth, such as the late 1980s, early 2000s and in 2006. The UK has the third largest current account deficit in the world after the USA and Spain. As the dollar has been falling against the pound, this deficit may be expected to worsen, but as the slowdown is exported from the USA to the global economy, the current account is likely to see a degree of self-correction. The pound has fallen against the euro, which is by far the most important trading currency for the UK, and this is likely to lessen the deficit.

The distribution of income described on the national statistics website (go to UK Snapshots on **www.statistics.gov.uk**, then type 'income distribution' in the search box) shows a widening during periods of economic growth, but other factors that help to explain this uneven distribution include accelerating wages at the top end of the scale, a fall in male participation in the workforce, meaning an increasing number of workless households, and changes in the tax and benefit system.

Perhaps the least achieved government objective is the protection of the environment. Clear and unambiguous indications are given in national statistics on carbon emissions. The Kyoto Protocol, ratified by 170 countries (but excluding the USA), states that by 2012 the developed countries will reach carbon emission levels 5% below their 1990 levels. Although the UK has seen some improvement, it is not on target. The EU Emissions Trading Scheme system set up in 2005 has yet to lead to carbon reduction, but as the prices of permits rise this situation should improve.

While each of these objectives can have serious effects on economic agents if it is out of control, some clearly have a more immediate impact on people's lives. For instance, unemployment not only means lost income, but can mean a long-term reduction in a person's employability through loss of skills and training. However, it might be that the government cannot solve unemployment in the short term. Many economists believe that too much cushioning of the unemployed results in an inefficient labour market, and that competition and increased incentives for those out of work are a better approach to dealing with unemployment.

Similarly, inflation of 2% is not thought to be a problem, and as long as incomes move in line with inflation there will be no serious side-effects. Most people's wages, and also student grants and pensions, are adjusted in line with inflation, and so reducing inflation below this level is not a priority. However, as inflation rises there comes a point where it erodes international competitiveness, discourages foreign inward investment, and causes income redistribution away from savers to borrowers to such a degree that its destabilising effects become a major concern.

A current account deficit on the balance of payments is of no concern to governments if there is enough trust in the capital markets and the value of the currency. It is, however, a sign that the country may be overspending relative to its income and at some point the outflow of money will have to be compensated by inflows. The UK has international investments abroad with enormous earning potential, which may mean that the balance will be restored if the situation is left to itself (**laissez faire**). Many economists therefore think that the UK government should not try to rectify a current account deficit with demand management. However, most agree that supply-side policies should be used to restore competitiveness in the long run.

43

Perhaps the most contentious of policy objectives is the idea of taxing the rich and giving to the poor. Social spending by the UK government on income support accounts for about a third of government expenditure — five times the amount spent on defence. Many would argue that redistributing income from the rich to the poor through taxes and benefits is simply unfair, destroys incentives and reduces the work ethic. The main drawback with social expenditure is that it has little effect on reducing poverty; some argue that it can even create a 'dependency culture'. While this might be true in general, extreme poverty is debilitating and leaves potential workers caught in a cycle of worklessness. They may be unable to sustain permanent employment at the available rates of pay due to personal circumstance, dependants, a lack of skills or the high cost of housing.

### Examination skills and concepts

- The priority given to the six macroeconomic objectives depends on the political stance of any particular government
- The aim of government is often not to reach a zero rate of, say, unemployment or inflation, as this would cause increased pressures elsewhere in the economy. It usually seeks a balance between the objectives. See the section on 'Conflicts between objectives', pp. 44–47.

### Common examination errors

- The government does not itself finance a deficit on the balance of payments. A deficit could, however, cause a fall in the UK banking system's reserves of foreign currency and result in a downward movement in the value of the currency — it is only in this respect that the government aims to maintain a balance, if at all.

### Useful exercises

- Look at the UK fact sheets available at **www.esrc.ac.uk** — this respected academic research institution is a valuable resource for the whole A-level course. Follow the 'facts and figures' link — the 'UK fact sheets' are within this. There are pages on productivity and distribution of wealth, to name just two.
- To see a breakdown of government spending, go to **www.hm-treasury.gov.uk**, access the webpage for the latest budget, click on the 'summary of key points' and look at the final page showing where taxpayers' money is spent.

### Links and common themes

- These objectives are revisited in more depth when considering the role of the state in Unit 4.

## Conflicts between objectives

In this section a limited range of conflicts have been chosen, although for each objective there are issues with every other objective. Some objectives, such as growth and employment, have more in common than others, such as growth and the environment. The degree to which there is conflict is a useful way to approach your evaluation.

## Inflation and unemployment

Consider this scenario. You are running a nightclub and the DJ is asking you for a wage increase. She may be good at the job, but you are not keen to pay more for the same service because it will eat into profits. What do you do? If there were a whole selection of unemployed DJs eager and willing to take up the post, you would probably look to employ a replacement, at the same or possibly at a lower rate than your current DJ. If, however, DJs are in short supply and the success of your club depends on having a good DJ whom you can rely on, you would be more likely to enter into discussion with your current DJ to keep her on board.

In other words, a shortage of labour in a specific field can cause wage pressures to build up. The net effect in the wider economy is that, as wages go up, people start spending more, the costs of production increase because labour is a major production cost, and inflation begins to rise. In other words, low unemployment or reduced spare capacity leads to higher inflation.

This basic analysis is the rationale for the **Phillips curve**, which was an observation of an apparent trade-off between unemployment and inflation (measured by the rate of change in wages) in the UK between 1861 and 1913.

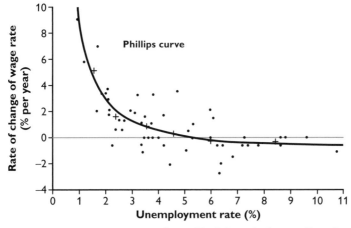

Source: 'The Relationship between Unemployment the Rate of Change of Money Wages, 1861–1957', *Economica* (1958)

***The relationship between inflation and unemployment in the UK, 1861–1913***

In practice, if a government starts trying to exploit this trade-off it is unlikely to have the desired result. For example, because of the transparency of a government's actions, if it tries to spend its way into reducing unemployment, the most likely effect will be an increase in wages to absorb the government's extra spending: that is, inflation. As inflation goes up, newly employed workers will soon realise that their wages are being eroded by inflation, and firms will realise that they are not getting as much profit out of their workers because of inflation; therefore any increase in employment is not likely to last in the long term. For these reasons, while the Phillips curve is an observable phenomenon, it is not necessarily a viable tool for a government.

### Economic growth and the balance of payments on the current account

As an economy grows and incomes rise, consumers are likely to demand more imports and firms' incentives to export will diminish, as it is easier to find eager customers in the domestic market. Therefore economic growth is likely to worsen the current account. The main exception to this is export-led growth, where the driver of growth is an increase in the export component of aggregate demand. Export-led growth means that the balance of payments will improve as more goods and services are sold abroad.

A second reason why growth might not necessarily worsen the balance of payments is if the growth is caused by an increase in aggregate supply. For example, owing to decreases in costs or increases in investment, an economy will become more internationally competitive, meaning that the economy can export more and import less while growing.

### Increased employment and the sustainable environment

If more workers are being employed, there is likely to be more congestion on the roads and more carbon use because of more offices, more manufacture and greater energy usage. In addition, as people's incomes increase, workers are more likely to go abroad for their holidays, and most foreign travel will involve increased carbon emissions.

On the other hand, higher employment can mean that the government has more scope for taxation, and one spin-off might be the opportunity to use 'green' taxes, where taxation is specifically designed to reduce carbon use. For example, in the March 2008 budget the first year of road tax was doubled for new 'gas-guzzling' vehicles. The effect of higher employment also depends on whether the increase is in the manufacturing or service sector. As more people can work remotely in the service sector, it may be that an increase in employment has a negligible effect on the environment.

### Economic growth and income redistribution

When an economy grows, incomes are most likely to rise at the top end of the income spectrum: for example, in the form of bonuses for sales executives. The effect is a widening of income inequality. However, over time, people at the high-income end of the scale may employ people from lower income groups, such as domestic staff. Increased demand for low-skilled labour should eventually lead to increased wages.

Nevertheless, many critics argue that, while there may be some transferred benefits of growth, there is a two-track labour market and those with low skills rarely benefit because, as skill shortages develop, immigration fills the gaps and the wages of low-skilled workers don't rise. Another counter-argument is that, even if wages rise by a constant percentage for everyone, income inequality will still increase in absolute terms.

### Inflation and equilibrium on the balance of payments

Low inflation should help to improve a balance of payments deficit on current account. Low prices relative to other countries will mean that exports become more attractive on world markets and imports are less attractive. However, if the balance of payments tends to be in surplus, control of inflation will not restore equilibrium in the sense of removing a surplus.

Furthermore, when one of the main objectives of macroeconomic policy is to control inflation, interest rates might be tighter than they would otherwise be. High interest rates often mean that the exchange rate rises: 'hot money' flows in, as funds move between international capital markets seeking the best interest and exchange rates. A strong currency makes a country's exports less competitive and its imports relatively cheap, worsening the trade position.

### Examination skills and concepts

- The Phillips curve is an empirical observation that there is a negative correlation between inflation (via money wages) and unemployment.
- The Phillips curve is used by some to argue that there is a trade-off between unemployment and inflation, and that if an economy can tolerate increased inflation then there would be lower long-term unemployment.
- Trade-offs can also be seen to exist between the other government macroeconomic objectives.

### Common examination errors

- While most candidates can draw and label a Phillips curve, few can explain why inflation would fall when unemployment rises, and vice versa.

### Links and common themes

- There is a link with the externalities analysis in Unit 1, and the role of the state in Unit 4.

# Policy instruments

## Demand-side policies

**Demand-side policy** is a deliberate manipulation by the government of aggregate demand in order to achieve macroeconomic objectives. There are two demand-side policies: **fiscal policy**, which is the government's management of its spending and taxation with the aim of changing the total level of spending in the economy; and **monetary policy**, which is decision making using monetary instruments such as the interest rate.

### Fiscal policy

If government spending is greater than taxation, the government is operating a **fiscal** or **budget deficit**. The net effect is to pump spending power into the economy. The **multiplier** magnifies the effect of this boost. So, for example, if the government builds a new hospital and does not pay for it all through current taxation, but instead borrows to finance the scheme, there will effectively be more spending power in the economy at the expense of spending power in the future. When the government pays for the workers and building materials for this hospital, the incomes will be re-spent in the economy, creating new incomes — which is the multiplier in operation. If an economy is going through a slowdown or a recession, then according to Keynesian thinking, the government should spend its way out of the recession.

By contrast, if government spending is less than taxation, there is said to be a **fiscal** or **budget surplus**, which takes spending power out of the economy with negative multiplier effects. The consensus among economists is that in times of boom or fast growth in the economy, the government should rein in its spending to curb inflationary pressures. This is known as **contractionary fiscal policy**, and it puts the government's accounts in a better position.

### *Does fiscal policy work?*
In the UK fiscal policy can only be implemented in the annual budget, although there is some room for manoeuvre in the autumn pre-budget report. This creates a time lag in decision making for fiscal policy, added to which there is an implementation lag because many tax changes cannot begin until the start of the new fiscal year in April, sometimes 1 or 2 years ahead. This means that if the government tries to respond to current economic problems using fiscal policy, the effect will not become apparent until the economy has started to change tack in the normal course of the economic cycle. Furthermore, when a government deliberately sets out to expand its spending, people will try to cash in on this by increasing their pay demands, and the effect will be increased wages and costs, rather than expanded output.

Next, there are **crowding-out effects** of increased spending by governments. For example, if the government decides to build a new hospital, there is less scope for a private hospital in the vicinity providing essentially the same service. There is also crowding out in the sense that when the government runs a deficit it needs to raise finance which, in times when credit is less readily available, will stifle private initiative. However, it can be argued that expansionary fiscal policy simply causes inflation because the debt issued to finance the expansion, often Treasury bills, is so liquid that it acts like printing money. There are many other critiques of fiscal policy and these are explored in Unit 4.

## Monetary policy
The manipulation of monetary variables such as the interest rate has enormous implications across the whole economy. In the UK a group of up to nine economists forming the Bank of England's Monetary Policy Committee, whose sole purpose is the control of inflation, makes the interest rate decision independently of government. They meet at least once a month for a day and a half to examine evidence from across the country relating to inflationary pressures. They have a target for CPI inflation set for them by the chancellor of the exchequer, currently at 2% ±1%. If inflation falls outside the range of 1–3%, the governor of the Bank of England must write an open letter to the chancellor to explain why this has happened. In its first 10 years of operation, this

occurred only once when inflation reached 3.1% in March 2007, but has risen signif-icantly above 3% since May 2008.

### Causes of inflation

In order to understand how monetary policy works it is important to consider the causes of inflation. In terms of *AD/AS* analysis, inflation can be shown as a shift to the right in *AD* or a shift to the left in *AS*. A shift to the right in *AD* is often called **demand pull inflation** and it occurs whenever *AD* shifts to the right, usually exacer-bated by multiplier effects. A shift to the left in *AS* is known as **cost push inflation** and occurs whenever costs of production increase in an economy. These might be for short-term reasons, such as a fall in the exchange rate making imports more expensive, or for longer term reasons such as higher corporation taxes.

However, according to monetarists such as Milton Friedman, inflation is 'always and everywhere a monetary phenomenon' (*Monetary History of the United States 1867–1960*, 1963). That is, monetarists believe that inflation is caused by increases in the money supply about the rate of the increase in the real output in the economy. Inflation can be controlled by controlling the money supply, either directly or more effectively perhaps through the rate of interest.

### Costs and benefits of inflation

Monetary policy involves controlling inflation, whether too high or too low. To judge whether the policy is worth pursuing it is helpful to consider the costs of inflation and possible benefits of a little inflation.

The costs of inflation include:
- **Loss of international competitiveness.** Exports become relatively expensive and imports relatively cheap. The balance of payments is likely to worsen.
- **Redistribution of income.** Those on fixed incomes will find incomes fall in real terms. Those with index-linked incomes will not lose out, unless linked to a fairly unrepresentative measure such as the CPI.
- **Increased uncertainty.** If firms think that costs are rising and fear increases in interest rates, they might curb investment.
- **Investment from abroad might decrease.** Inflation erodes the value of money, so why buy into a currency that is falling in value?

Benefits of inflation might include:
- **Inflation reduces the real interest rate**, so cost of borrowing falls. Also, those with large debts such as mortgages find the real value of the debt will fall.
- Increased prices might be a sign that **firms can make more profits**. So in contrast to the above point about uncertainty, it might mean that investment is encouraged
- A little inflation provides a cushion against the perils of **deflation**. When prices are falling the economy can run into a vicious circle of underinvestment and spending.
- A little inflation means that **real wage differentials can be changed** without actually cutting money wages. The argument is that people will accept wage rises below the rate of inflation but will never accept wage cuts.

### How monetary policy works

When interest rates are raised, the cost of borrowing rises. Consumers who borrow in order to finance their spending might be deterred from doing so and savers will be less keen to spend their savings because there is a greater opportunity cost in so doing. People with mortgages — of whom there are almost 10 million in the UK — will find their mortgage interest repayments rise, and will therefore be discouraged from spending, although those with fixed-rate mortgages will not suffer this immediately. Hire purchase — the method of buying major durable items, such as cars and white goods, on credit — will incur increasingly expensive monthly repayment instalments, which means that consumers might delay further major expenditures. House prices may fall as mortgages become less affordable, and this can cause negative wealth effects, where lower asset prices mean that people feel less inclined to spend and less able to take out loans based on the equity in their homes.

Firms will find that investment is less attractive in many cases, and that fewer investments will make a return higher than the increased cost of borrowing. Therefore, firms will be less inclined to invest, which not only reduces current aggregate demand, but also has implications for long-term output prospects. The cost of exports might increase because interest rates are essentially a cost of production, so exports will fall and imports will rise. This is made even more likely when we factor in a very probable increase in the exchange rate, which occurs when 'hot' money is attracted to higher interest rates in the UK.

All these changes shift the *AD* curve to the left with multiplier effects. Depending on the shape of the *AS* curve, this may decrease both the price level and real output. Increasing interest rates can be an effective way of controlling inflation, but the cost is that economic growth also falls.

### How effective is monetary policy?

Monetary policy has a shorter time lag than fiscal policy, although the Monetary Policy Committee estimates that interest rate changes can take 18 months to 2 years to have their full impact. There are further time delays because many mortgage holders have fixed-rate policies, which may delay the impact on their spending for some years. Furthermore, monetary policy is a very blunt tool that hits the whole economy, affecting both small and large firms, and rises in interest rates usually worsen income distribution. But perhaps the most significant criticism of monetary policy is that it raises costs of production in a situation where the cause of inflation may itself be an increase in costs. So the rise in interest rates, rather than curing the problem, exacerbates it. In a time of rising commodity prices, the people who have to bear the brunt of this are those who have debts.

content guidance

## Supply-side policies

**Supply-side policies** include any action by the government intended to increase the amount that firms are willing to supply at any given price level. In other words, they seek to shift the aggregate supply curve to the right.

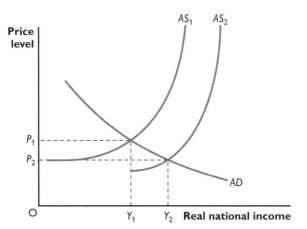

*Effect of an increase in aggregate supply*

There are three basics ways of achieving this:

- **Increasing price flexibility and signalling in a market.** If prices are not used to allocate resources effectively, there will be surpluses or deficits in the market. Suppose the government failed to increase the real rate of the minimum wage: this means that real wages would fall and there would be less unemployment in the labour market. Firms' real costs of production would therefore go down, and the *AS* curve would shift to the right.
- **Increasing competition.** Reducing artificial constraints such as legal monopoly rights, as in the UK Post Office, can increase competition. As firms compete, they must either cut costs or become more innovative in order to survive, which effectively shifts the *AS* curve to the right by reducing costs. Another way to increase competition is to privatise, although there is little scope left for privatisation of publicly owned firms in the UK. Deregulation is another option — this happened in the 1980s in the UK with the freeing up of the bus and coach operations sector.
- **Improving incentives.** Incentives function by giving people higher rewards for what they do, and therefore motivating them to work harder. The most obvious way to do this is to cut marginal tax rates. Longer-term solutions involve improving health, education and training, introducing performance-related pay and reducing corporation tax, which is a tax on a firm's profits. Again, these will encourage firms to produce more at any given price level.

### How effective are supply-side policies?

While some supply-side policies are clearly very effective — for example, deregulation in the phone industry has resulted in greatly improved standards in terms of price levels, after-care service and the like — there are some industries in which there is either no opportunity for increased competition, or where the benefits are outweighed by increased costs. For example, many believe that increased competition in the NHS has merely resulted in increased management costs rather than improved efficiency.

Another issue with supply-side policies is again the time lag. Some policies, most notably in education, can take many years to have any effect on production costs. If anything, in the short run they increase costs because there are fewer people in the labour market.

In addition, supply-side policies have side-effects on the demand side. For example, cutting taxes will have fiscal policy implications. Perhaps the most important aspect is that cutting minimum real wages and reducing trade union power affects lower-income earners adversely and disproportionately. However, effective supply-side policies do have the benign outcome of both lower inflation and higher rates of economic growth.

### Examination skills and concepts

- Demand-side policies are used to shift the *AD* curve. They include fiscal and monetary policies.
- Supply-side policies are used to increase the aggregate supply in an economy.
- Most governments use a combination of both types of policy to stabilise prices and maintain growth rates in the economy.

### Common examination errors

- The Monetary Policy Committee has a single target: inflation. It is incorrect to say that it aims to reduce unemployment or indeed has any other macroeconomic policy objective.

### Useful exercises

- Read the minutes of the latest Monetary Policy Committee meeting at **www.bankofengland.co.uk**. List eight factors it has taken into account in making its interest rate decision, showing in each case how these relate to the price level in the UK.

### Links and common themes

- In taking this subject further in Unit 4, you will gain a more international perspective on these issues.

## Do macroeconomic policies conflict?

### Fiscal policy and supply-side policy

Increased government spending may be used as part of a fiscal policy to increase aggregate demand, and much of this spending will be directed to the health and education sectors. In this case, fiscal and supply-side policies are working in tandem to improve growth prospects, and the supply-side effects may cancel out any ill effects on the price level from the expansion in demand.

By contrast, if a government is using contractionary fiscal policy as a means of trying to control the price level, the impact might be a leftward shift of the *AS* curve, and therefore prices might rise rather than fall and output might contract even further than intended.

### Fiscal and monetary policy

While these are both demand-side policies, if a government runs a budget deficit, this has to be financed, which will affect the money markets. Much of the budget deficit is financed by issuing government 3-month Treasury bills, which offer investors secure and liquid assets that are easy to trade on the money markets. This helps with stability during a credit crunch, but at other times it might be inflationary because it increases liquidity available. A looser fiscal policy can mean that the Monetary Policy Committee favours a tighter monetary policy, taking into account the fiscal stance in deciding whether to raise interest rates.

### Monetary policy and supply-side policy

A tight monetary policy means that interest rates are higher than they perhaps need to be. While this may control inflation, it increases costs for firms if they are borrowing money. By contrast, raising interest rates tends to make exchange rates rise. As UK firms import nearly all their raw materials, the effect on production costs may be significant. Therefore tight monetary policy can instead improve the supply side, although higher exchange rates are not guaranteed and they do harm firms trying to export. In the case of cutting interest rates, as in loose monetary policy, this can reduce borrowing costs for domestic firms, but if the exchange rate falls, firms will face increased import costs but gain competitiveness internationally.

**Examination skills and concepts**

- Some analysts doubt that expansionary fiscal policy has any positive effects at all.
- Monetary policy is clearly powerful in controlling aggregate demand, but it is a blunt tool and has damaging effects on income distribution and across the supply side of the economy.
- Supply-side policies are now rather limited in their potential in the UK, and can cost a great deal for the government in terms of fiscal policy. However, policies aimed at increasing investment in the economy can have benefits in the future despite fiscal implications in the short run.
- A fiscal deficit means that the government needs to borrow from the money markets. This can produce two very different side-effects, depending on the type of credit available in the money markets. If there is a shortage of long-term funds, there may be crowding out as the government can offer good terms and security. But if money is lacking liquidity and the government borrows short term, issuing Treasury bills is a little like printing more money. This effectively loosens the money markets, which can be inflationary.

**Common examination errors**

- Many answers mistake the impact of a change in the interest rate on the exchange rate. Usually they move in the same direction.

## Useful exercises

- Look in the *Financial Times* for the prices of Treasury bills. Note that they do not earn interest — instead they are issued at a discount on their redemption price. Choose a bond and work out what the interest is: work out the discount on the time left before it is redeemed, then make this into an annual figure.
- Visit the website of the Institute for Fiscal Studies (**www.ifs.org.uk**) or the National Institute of Economic and Social Research (**www.niesr.ac.uk**), where you can get access to a simulation model of the whole economy on the web. You can then be your own chancellor, put in extra public spending, track the change in national income over time and see the multiplier at work.

## Links and common themes

- You do not need an in-depth understanding of money markets, but there are links with the way shares work (Unit 1) and with the significance of public sector borrowing (Unit 4).

# Questions
# &
# Answers

This section contains four data-response questions with student responses and examiner's comments that are designed to help you improve your understanding and examination technique. By seeing common examination errors in practice you can learn to avoid the common pitfalls. The student answers are graded A to C, with examiner's comments preceded by the icon *e* to indicate where all the extra marks could be found.

In the examination, you will have 90 minutes and you will have to choose one from a choice of two questions. You should spend 10 minutes reading and choosing the question, giving you 1 minute per mark to earn a total of 80 marks. There is nothing worse than getting halfway through a question and realising that you would have been able to respond better to the other question.

Some questions are marked with an asterisk (*). This indicates that the quality of written communication will be taken into account by the examiner. The way that this is done is to award the balance of any doubt to the candidate in cases where an answer is expressed with clarity, but not in cases where there is obscurity in the response.

# Indicators of economic performance

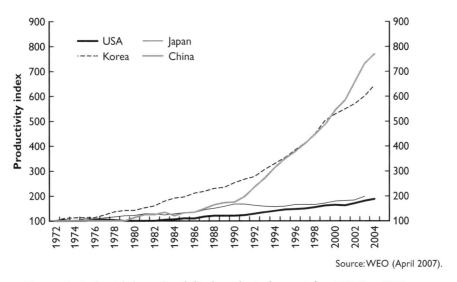

Source: WEO (April 2007).

*Figure 1  Industrial productivity in selected countries (1972 = 100)*

Source: UN Human Development Report http://hdrstats.undp.org/countries/country_fact_sheet

*Figure 2  HDI and GDP per head for two countries, 2005*

Table 1 *Selected measures of economic performance, 2007 values*

| | GDP per capita (purchasing power parities, US$) | Life expectancy (years) | Human Development Index |
|---|---|---|---|
| USA | 41,890 | 77.9 | 0.951 |
| Japan | 31,267 | 82.3 | 0.953 |
| Republic of Korea | 22,029 | 77.9 | 0.921 |
| China | 6,757 | 72.5 | 0.777 |

Source: United Nations Human Development Report, 2007/08.

(a) **Refer to Figure 1.**
  (i) **Explain what is meant by the term *industrial productivity*.** (4 marks)
  (ii) **Using an example from the data, explain what is meant by 1972 = 100.** (4 marks)
  (iii) **Using an appropriate diagram, explain the likely effect of the change in productivity on the level of aggregate supply and the price level in a country such as China.** (10 marks)

(b) **Using the data in Figure 2:**
  (i) **Outline one advantage and one disadvantage of using HDI figures to measure standards of living.** (8 marks)
  (ii) **Assess two possible reasons why Japan and the USA have similar rankings for the Human Development Index, but are widely different for GDP at purchasing power parity.** (12 marks)
  (iii) **HDI is a measure of economic development. Apart from HDI, examine the relative merits of two measures of economic development.** (12 marks)

*(c) **Seven out of the world's ten most polluting cities are in China. Assess the benefits and costs of growth for a country such as China, using the information provided in Figures 1 and 2 and Table 1.** (30 marks)

■ ■ ■

## Candidate's answer

**(a) (i)** Output per unit of input in the industrial or 'secondary' sector. It includes manufacturing and construction. It ignores productivity in areas such as farming (primary) and services (tertiary). **4/4 marks**

> Definition questions must always be brief but precise. Productivity must be distinguished from 'production' by looking at factor inputs as well as output, so use of the phrase 'per unit of input' makes this a good answer. Data reference would be advised, but marks are not reserved for this, as they are in the following question.

**(ii)** 1972 has been chosen as the base year. This is used to make comparisons. Base years are often chosen because they are fairly typical, and there were not any great distortions. **2/4 marks**

🖉 This shows adequate understanding of the concept, but there has been no reference to the data. The next step might have been to say that US industrial productivity has doubled since 1972 while in China it is almost eight times as high as it was in 1972.

**(iii)** Increased productivity lowers the costs of production for firms because they can produce more output for the same factor costs. Aggregate supply increases, and price levels should fall. This is because China has seen enormous rises in productivity. **10/10 marks**

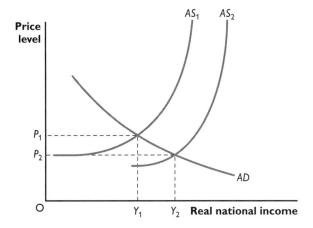

🖉 The shift is described correctly, and the word 'costs' is used, which is crucial for AS questions. There is an attempt to apply the concept to China, and to use the evidence provided in Figure 1. Four marks are earned for a fully labelled diagram. It shows the new and old price level — a detail that the examiner will be looking for. In cases such as this where the question is fully addressed, full marks will be given despite the brevity of the response.

**(b) (i)** Advantage: HDI stands for the Human Development Index. The advantage of HDI is that it does combine the effects of increased growth with other quality of life indicators, and in that respect is an important measure of development. It might be worth comparing the HDI with other measures, some of which contain a GDP element and some that don't.

Disadvantage: This index does not take account of poverty or other measures of deprivation, and in that respect is regarded by some as being of limited value. **4/8 marks**

🖉 The content of this answer is accurate but a little wordy. There are no marks available for stating what HDI stands for, and there is opportunity cost in so doing. It would be better to say more about the advantages and disadvantages as requested. For example, the HDI is a better measure of living standards than income alone, in that it takes into account health and education as well as the use of PPP values per head in real terms. School enrolment and life expectancy are among the most reliable indicators, providing data that are fairly easy to access and comparable across different countries.

The main disadvantage could refer to 'income distribution', or a sense of the quality of education or the extra years lived. Political oppression or loss of a homeland is not measured, for example.

**(ii)** Table 1 gives one main reason. The Japanese have a lower income per head but the life expectancy at 82.3 years is almost 5 years longer than the people in the USA.

The other possible reason is school enrolment. Although it is not shown in the table, it is probably the case that the Japanese school enrolment is higher than in the USA. **8/12 marks**

This is a good answer in that both reasons employ sound economics, and there is reference to the data. The only thing the answer lacks is evaluation. The answer could weigh up which is more likely: whether the data could be inaccurate, or whether things could change over time — for example, Japan's income per head might be about to fall.

**(iii)** One measure is GDP. This is the measure of total incomes in a country. If incomes go up then people are likely to enjoy higher standards of living which is a part of economic development. But this is not a very useful measure unless it is given 'per head' or in real values (taking out the effects of inflation). Also it doesn't take into account the cost of living. **3/6 marks**

GDP is arguably not a measure of economic development, although changes in real GDP per head might mean a change in development. So this is an unwise choice, although some credit is given for the evaluation.

Another measure is number of mobile phones per thousand of the population. With a mobile phone a farmer can get produce or a fisherman can get the catch to the market with the best price. Mobile phones act as a banking tool (for example, credit on phones can be used for trade) and can solve problems of poor credit in developing countries. Access to a mobile phone for a community can mean that health services can be accessed in an emergency. Mobiles transform the lives of people in a developing economy, so this may be one of the most important measures of development, and it is a better measure than landlines which are not so versatile owing to the need for a wider infrastructure. **6/6 marks**

The mobile phone measure is perfectly acceptable and well explained, and the candidate attempts to evaluate by saying it is has advantages relative to another measure: that is, prioritisation with justification.

**\*(c)** One benefit of growth is that incomes are rising, and if incomes are rising, people are likely to have higher standards of living. Economic growth is one of the six macroeconomic objectives of governments, and growth has two main causes. The causes of growth are a shift to the right in the *AD* and a shift to the right in the *AS*. *AD* might rise because consumption, investment, government spending or exports have risen, or because saving, taxes or imports have fallen. There is a multiplier effect. *AS* might rise because there is a fall in investment, a fall in production costs such as wages, or a rise in the exchange rate making imports cheaper.

The benefits of growth for consumers are that they can buy more goods and services with their higher incomes, or they could have longer holidays and shorter working hours. Benefits for the government are that it receives higher tax revenue (this assumes that the tax thresholds remain the same) and this means that it is easier for the government to make income distribution more equal by the 'Robin Hood' process of taxing the rich to give to the poor. Firms also benefit because they have higher profits (because they sell more) and even the environment might improve because rich countries that have signed the Kyoto agreement of 1997 are committed to using cleaner and greener methods of production, and these methods cost money which the increased income from the growth can pay for through an increase in tax revenues.

The costs of growth are the environmental damage. More production means more pollution and depletion of natural resources. Also, income distribution might not get better because it tends to be the rich people who get richer quicker when the economy is growing, whereas people like cleaners get paid the same. Also, higher incomes usually involve longer workings hours, not shorter ones. **12/30 marks**

🖉 This student has made a classic error in starting with the *causes* rather than the *effects* of growth. While this does not lose the candidate any marks, nor does it gain any, there is an opportunity cost in that less time can be devoted to relevant material. The candidate has listed the standard points for and against the benefits and costs of growth, but the evaluation is limited. It is clear from the answer that there are two sides to every point, but it would be better to discuss the advantages and disadvantages of each point in turn and come to a reasoned conclusion.

The most important evaluation point is that the effects might be different in the short run and the long run. For example, although economic growth often makes income distribution worse in the short run, these incomes might even out over time as the 'rich' spend their money, with multiplier effects. A second evaluation point might be that the effect on the environment might be difficult to measure, and it depends on whether the growth is based in the industrial or services sector. In the latter case, the environmental aspects will not be so significant.

To summarise, the candidate would score well on analysis marks but is lacking application and evaluation.

**Total score: 49/80 = grade C**

# Question 2

# Food and oil prices

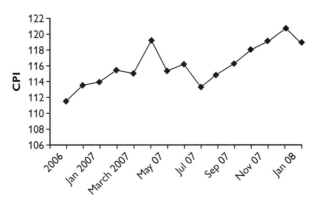

*Figure 1   Consumer price index (food) in the UK (2000 = 100)*

*Table 1   Oil price changes in pounds and dollars (Brent crude)*

| Currency | Percentage change on previous month | | | | |
|---|---|---|---|---|---|
| | 2007 | | | | 2008 |
| | Sep | Oct | Nov | Dec | Jan |
| Pounds | 8.2 | 5.9 | 10.9 | 1.2 | **3.1** |
| Dollars | 8.6 | 7.3 | 12.3 | −1.5 | **0.9** |

Source: www.bankofengland.co.uk

(a) Refer to Figure 1.
   (i) Using Figure 1, calculate the percentage change in the food price
       index between July 2007 and January 2008.                          (4 marks)
   (ii) Assess the likely impact on UK income distribution when food
        prices rise.                                                       (12 marks)

(b) Making reference to Table 1:
   (i) Explain what happened to oil prices in December 2007 in both
       pounds and dollars.                                                 (4 marks)
   (ii) Outline one likely reason for this difference.                     (4 marks)
   (iii) With the aid of an aggregate demand and supply diagram, analyse
         the likely impact on the UK's real output and price level of the
         trend in oil prices over the period from July 2007 to January 2008.   (16 marks)

(c) Apart from food and oil prices, explain two factors that the Bank of
    England's Monetary Policy Committee considers when it makes its
    interest rate decision.                                                (10 marks)

*(d) **Discuss the likely effects on the price level in the UK if interest rates are raised. Consider the impact on the economy of a change in the exchange rate in your answer.**

(30 marks)

■ ■ ■

## Candidate's answer

**(a) (i)**    $120 - 114 = 6$                                                                          **1/4 marks**

The candidate has selected the correct years and read the data accurately from the graph, but the formula for percentage change is always change/original × 100, which in this case is $6/114 \times 100 = 5.3\%$.

**(ii)**    Everybody needs food and rich people probably spend more on food than poor people, so I would guess that income distribution doesn't change much, if it improves at all. However, it depends which food gets more expensive. If it's fast food it might affect poor people more, but if it's caviar it would affect rich people more.                                                                **5/12 marks**

The important piece of analysis that the student omitted is that food accounts for a larger proportion of the spending of lower-income groups. Therefore, rising food prices mean that lower-income groups have less money to spend after food has been paid for. However, the gross income remains unaffected unless you want to argue that rising food prices somehow reduce the gross income of lower-income groups; it would be better to argue in the evaluation that the income distribution changes *after* food costs have been taken into account.

From the brevity of the answer it is clear that the candidate is on unsure ground. If you are uncertain, it is unwise to tell the examiner you are guessing; instead, follow through your ideas with reasons as far as you can. This is an evaluative question because more than one answer can be given. The student clearly recognises this and gains marks for attempting to evaluate.

**(b) (i)**    In pounds they rose by 1.2% but in dollars they fell by 1.5%.            **4/4 marks**

Data are selected correctly and the answer makes it clear that one is rising and one is falling.

**(ii)**    Obviously the pound got stronger.                                                          **1/4 marks**

If something is 'obvious', it usually follows that it is not worth asking a question about. It is true that the pound has probably gained in strength against the dollar, but it might be that the dollar fell, or the dollar and the pound fell with the dollar falling faster. The key point is that the exchange rate between the pound and the dollar has strengthened and the dollar will buy fewer units of oil. For 2 marks there needs to be reference to the exchange rate, not just the pound, and for the other 2 marks there must be some reference to the data.

**question**

**(iii)** The UK is a net importer of food and oil. Although we produce both, we buy more in value terms from abroad than we export. When prices of these commodities go up, the response by consumers is very small — in other words there is low price-elasticity of demand. When PED is less than 1, a rise in prices means that total expenditure rises, so when the prices of these goods go up, total expenditure on imports rises. Imports are a component of *AD* (aggregate demand) and therefore *AD* falls. This effect is made more extreme by the multiplier effect.

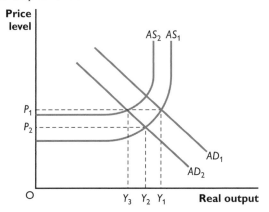

The increase in commodity prices also affects aggregate supply, which in a sense is the cost of production. All producers need oil and food in the UK and therefore all firms' costs will rise, therefore *AS* shifts to the left, prices rise and output falls.

Overall the price effects might outweigh each other, but the output effects will reinforce each other (return to $P_1$), and we would expect a fall or a slowdown in real output $Y_3$. **16/16 marks**

This answer includes the multiplier and an accurate diagram, and covers both the *AD* and *AS* sides of the case. Most answers will give only the *AS* side and this one stands out as far better than the average.

**(c)** First factor: The MPC (Monetary Policy Committee) takes into account the current account of the balance of payments. If there is a deficit such as the one the UK is currently experiencing (£45 billion) this is a sign that the UK economy is spending more than it is selling abroad, and it might be that the pound will fall in the future, which is inflationary (imports become more expensive). However, the deficit itself is not inflationary and therefore the MPC is unlikely to be worried directly by a deficit. In fact, if $X - M$ is less than zero there is a negative effect on *AD*, which *reduces* inflationary pressure. **5/5 marks**

This is an ideal answer. The current account is one of the many thousands of factors looked at by the Monetary Policy Committee when making its interest rate decision. A deficit may mean that inflation will not hit the target. The answer stresses the role of the MPC and the inflation target, and gives real-world evidence.

Second factor: The MPC looks very carefully at house prices. If house prices are falling, as they were during the autumn of 2007, this can mean that there is a negative wealth effect. In the USA this triggered a credit crunch, and interest rates have had to fall dramatically to try to keep demand up. If demand is falling there will be unemployment. **3/5 marks**

📝 This is a common approach to this type of question, and it starts off well. By focusing on some real data and the concept of wealth effects, the answer hits on an important area of concern for the Monetary Policy Committee. But then no link is made to inflation, and instead the answer heads off to talk about unemployment, which may well be an important consideration for the government but is of no concern to the MPC.

**\*(d)** If interest rates are raised there will be an impact on most of the components of aggregate demand, $C + I + G + (X - M)$. First we look at consumption ($C$). $C$ falls for many reasons. One is that savings become more attractive and loans become more expensive. People will be less inclined to take money out of savings to spend, and will be less inclined to borrow if they have a choice about their spending. For example, a person might choose to delay buying a car. Also people will find things bought on hire purchase will have higher monthly instalments, so they will be less inclined to borrow in this way. Also $C$ falls because mortgage interest payments will increase so people will have less money left over to buy goods and services. Also people may feel less confident about the economy so they might rein back their spending plans. This would be especially true for people who have their own businesses and expect sales to fall.

Secondly, investment will also fall when interest rates rise. This is because the interest rate is the cost of borrowing money for investment, and only very profitable projects will be worth taking the risk of investing in when interest rates are too high.

Thirdly, $X - M$ will be likely to fall. This is for two reasons. The first is that we will export less (as firms face higher interest rates there are increased production costs) and imports will fall (we will suck in fewer imports because our spending is down). The second reason is that the pound is likely to rise. This is because hot money will be attracted to the pound as sterling bank accounts will be earning higher returns. With a 'Strong Pound Imports are Cheap and Exports are Dear' (SPICED). This means that $M$ will rise and $X$ will fall, so $AD$ will fall. This is made even more pronounced because of the multiplier.

$AD$ falls meaning prices will fall and output will fall.

The extent of the impact on the price levels depends on where on the $AS$ curve the $AD$ crosses. If $AS$ is very inelastic (the steep part), the impact on the price level will be very large. The economy will have very little spare capacity and there will be strong pressures to increase prices. A rise in the interest rate will relieve much of the pressure on prices as people stop spending, and the price level will fall significantly. However if the $AD$ crosses the more elastic part of the $AS$ curve, there

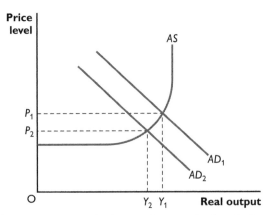

will be little effect on prices and a large effect on the level of output and probably employment in the country. Raising interest rates will just bring more gloom in an economy where there is a lot of spare capacity already, and people deciding to spend less will cause further stagnation in the economy.

Another evaluation point is that the interest rate impact does not always happen immediately. Many people have fixed rate mortgages, and even if mortgage interest payments do change, the mortgage holder might not react straight away. It is the same with the exchange rate. Even if the pound gets stronger, it probably won't make people stop buying things from the UK. If foreign tourists have booked their holidays already, they won't cancel if the pound gets stronger. They just might think more carefully about where they go in the future. This is a time lag, and it depends on the price elasticity of demand for exports and imports.                          **28/30 marks**

✐ An excellent analysis (18/18). There are just a couple of points to note on the analysis side: the SPICED acronym is really useful for you to remember the effect of a change in the exchange rate, but you don't want to tell the examiner about it. Secondly, the first point about $(X - M)$, with $X$ falling and $M$ rising due to changes in spending in the UK, is really a repeat of the argument about $C$, so it would have been better just to do the analysis concerning the change in the exchange rate, as indicated in the question.

The evaluation marks are 6/6 and 4/6. There is one very good piece of evaluation followed by a slightly less developed attempt. The candidate might have offered a third point: for example, that the pound is influenced by many things apart from the interest rates, or that relative interest rates are important, so the Fed and ECB rates need to be taken into account. Also in evaluation, if interest rates rise and AD slows, firms in the UK might look for new export markets to keep sales figures buoyant, so the balance of payments might not worsen as much. Then three pieces of evaluation could be awarded 4 + 4 + 4 and full marks would be awarded overall.

Overall, despite some very uncertain areas in the question as a whole, the candidate gets to an A by making sure that the longer answers pull up the grade.

**Total score: 63/80 = grade A**

# Income and wealth

### Table 1  House prices in the UK

| | Average house price | Index | Monthly change (%) | Annual change (%) |
|---|---|---|---|---|
| January 2008 | £229,625 | 233.8 | 0.1 | 6.5 |
| December 2007 | £229,496 | 233.7 | −0.2 | 7.4 |
| November 2007 | £230,031 | 234.2 | −0.1 | 8.9 |
| October 2007 | £230,284 | 234.5 | 0.6 | 9.8 |

Source: www.bankofengland.co.uk

### Extract 1  The international economy and UK GDP growth

International economic prospects have deteriorated since the November report. In the United States GDP growth fell sharply, the labour market weakened and the weakness in the housing market appeared to be spreading to other parts of the economy. As a result the Federal Reserve reduced official interest rates substantially. In the euro area business surveys pointed to some slowing in output growth from its recent firm pace. In contrast, the emerging market economies of Asia continued to expand robustly.

Overall, the Committee expects a modest slowing in the growth of the main UK export markets. That is offset by the depreciation of sterling, which can be expected to boost UK competitiveness.

Consequently net trade is expected to add to GDP growth over the next few years, contrary to the experience over much of the past decade.

GDP growth moderated to 0.6% in the fourth quarter according to preliminary estimates, with the slowdown concentrated in the financial and retail sectors. Business surveys and reports from the Bank's regional Agents point to a further modest slowdown in activity in early 2008.

Source: Bank of England, Inflation Report, February 2008, www.bankofengland.co.uk

(a) (i)   Describe what happened to house prices in December 2007.   (4 marks)

   (ii)  Outline the likely impact of this change in house prices on
         consumer expenditure. Refer to the *wealth effect* in your answer.   (6 marks)

   (iii) With reference to the information provided, evaluate the likely
         effects on the **UK** price level and equilibrium real output of the
         changes in incomes in the international economy.   (12 marks)

(b) (i)   With reference to Extract 1, explain what is meant by the
         term *injection*.   (6 marks)

   (ii)  Outline the mechanism by which a change in an injection can
         have a greater impact on total incomes in an economy.   (10 marks)

**question**

(c) Discuss the likely effect on the price level in the **UK** when interest rates fall in the **USA**. (12 marks)

*(d) To what extent is it likely that policies intended to increase economic growth will conflict with the working of other government policies? (30 marks)

■ ■ ■

## Candidate's answer

**(a) (i)** They rose by 7.4%. **0/4 marks**

The candidate was probably rushing and misread the data: 7.4% is the change between December 2006 and December 2007, but the change over the *month* was a fall of 0.2%.

**(ii)** When house prices go up, consumer expenditure goes up. This is because housing in the UK is the major form of asset held by consumers — almost half of everything they own. When the value of assets goes up, people holding them tend to feel better off, and therefore spend more. This is called a wealth effect. Rising house prices also mean that people can take out increased loans based on the increased value of their property, a process called equity release, and this again means that consumer expenditure may increase. **6/6 marks**

Although the candidate got the direction wrong for the change in house prices, he or she is not penalised again in this part of the question. This answer shows a good understanding of wealth effects (3/3) and gives two reasons why house price rises would lead to more spending. Another approach would be to refer to increased consumer confidence.

**(iii)** In the passage it says that the euro area and the USA are experiencing a slowdown in incomes, whereas Asian economies are growing and the overall impact is that UK exports are rising, albeit at a slowing rate. Increases in net exports will boost the circular flow in the UK which shifts the *AD* to the right.

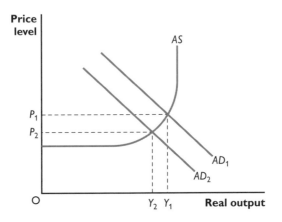

Price levels rise and output rises. However, the passage also states that the value of sterling is falling which 'can be expected to boost UK competitive-ness', so although exports are rising more slowly, the fall in the value of the pound will make exports increasingly cheap relative to other goods and services in the international economy, and imports relatively expensive. This might mean that *AD* increases at a faster rate. It all depends on the price-elasticity of demand for exports and imports. **8/12 marks**

*e* This succinct answer makes good use of the passage and provides clear analytical observations. However, in the diagram the *AD* shift is shown in the wrong direction and this means that the four easy diagram marks are missed. The evaluation is valid, but another point that could have been mentioned is that the UK does most of its trade (73%) with the euro area and this area will therefore have the most significant impact on the level of exports from the UK.

**(b) (i)** An injection is an input into the circular flow of income. Examples are investment, government spending and exports. When these rise, the circular flow of income rises because they are exogenous, that is, from outside the system. **4/6 marks**

*e* A textbook explanation of the term. However, there is no reference to Extract 1, where the report refers to exports.

**(ii)** The multiplier is a formula that relates an initial change in spending to the total change in spending that will result. A change in an injection has multi-plier effects. When, for example, exports increase there is a flow of money into the economy which is in a sense new money. It will become an income for the exporting firm which will then spend this money on paying the factors of production, for example wages. The workers who earn this money may spend it which means the money becomes someone else's income. These knock-on effects in the economy of a change in income will have a greatly magnified effect on incomes as a whole. The amount by which a change in the injection has a final impact depends on the size of the leakages. The leakages are savings, tax and imports. These take money out of the flow and reduce the multiplier effect. The bigger the leakages, the smaller the multi-plier. Eventually the multiplier process dies out as the extra spending of the economy leaks away. **10/10 marks**

*e* While the prose is not sophisticated, the ideas are expressed clearly and the mechanics of the multiplier are delivered effectively.

**(c)** When interest rates fall in the USA people in the USA will feel better off and will start spending more. One reason is because mortgage repayments will fall and they will have more money to spend on goods and services, some of which might be the UK's exports. Consumer spending might also rise because the Americans will save less and feel more confident about taking out loans. Therefore, American firms will find they can sell goods and services more easily in the USA and the incentive to sell goods and services to the UK will not be so strong. Therefore the UK will experience a rise in exports and a fall in imports. This will increase *AD*, so price levels in the UK will rise. Also, when interest rates fall in the USA the dollar will fall in value. This effectively means that the pound is stronger, and this means that the UK will find it more difficult to export and easier to import. These effects might outweigh each other, although I think the second argument is stronger. **10/12 marks**

> The analysis is secure and there is an attempt at evaluation by saying that 'effects might outweigh each other' and it depends on which is greater. However, when candidates use the personal pronoun and say 'I think…', it does little to convince the examiner; it would be better to spell out reasons why one effect might be greater than another.

*(d)* Policies intended to increase growth can be reflationary demand-side polices such as monetary and fiscal policy, or supply-side policies. Fiscal policy might be used to increase aggregate demand by increasing government spending (*G*) or cutting taxation (*T*). Monetary policy can be used to increase growth by cutting interest rates, although in the UK the Monetary Policy Committee does not aim to increase growth, it rather allows growth to occur by cutting interest rates when inflation falls below target. These shift *AD* to the right, and the effect on national income is magnified by the multiplier effect.

These policies are likely to conflict with the working of policies to improve the environment. Green taxes can be used to try to change the way people use goods and services with a high carbon use. Cutting taxes generally would mean that people have more money to drive large cars and fly to foreign countries for their holidays. The higher people's incomes become with economic growth, the less sensitive they are to green taxes. So even if cutting taxes in other areas outweighs the green taxes, the green taxes themselves will not have a very powerful environmental impact as the economy grows.

Supply-side policies are any action by the authorities to try to increase competition, incentives and the flexibility of the workforce. In the past they have included privatisation and deregulation, but they can also include tax cuts and legislation to reduce the power of the trade unions or cutting the national minimum wage. The aim is to shift the aggregate supply curve to the right. Costs will fall in the economy, and the equilibrium will occur at a higher rate of GDP.

However supply-side policies do have side-effects which might conflict with the workings of other government policies. For example, reducing the power of trade unions or cutting the national minimum wage is unlikely to improve the distribution of income. But in other ways the supply-side policies might improve the working of other policies such as monetary policy. As costs fall in the economy this will dampen inflationary pressures. And cutting taxes to improve incentives has a similar effect to expansionary fiscal policy. **26/30 marks**

📝 This answer covers the main policies effectively, and there are two good attempts at evaluation. The answer would gain full marks with the inclusion of a diagram showing how these policies affect price levels and real output, or the equivalent written explanation.

**Total score: 64/80 = grade A**

# Conflicts between fiscal policy and other government policy

### Extract 1

Two months after the proper budget, the government has unveiled what is, in effect, a mini-budget that will have a noticeable effect on the incomes of 22 million people.

Just eight weeks after Alistair Darling told MPs that there was not enough money to pay for large tax cuts, he has announced a £2.7 billion tax cut — hefty, by any standards, and far bigger than the very modest handout in the budget.

Having suggested that he would use the fiddly tax-credit system to compensate the people who lost out through the abolition of the 10 pence starting rate of tax, Darling has instead opted for a simple system that will see taxpayers getting extra money in their pay packets from September without them having to fill in a single new form.

And at a time when people are complaining bitterly about the impact of rising fuel and food prices, Brown and Darling have used the 10 pence row as an opportunity to spray money at 22 million people, 17 million more than were affected by the abolition of the 10 pence rate, in an attempt to ease some of the consumer pain.

In the USA George Bush's administration has been handing out tax rebates worth up to $600 (£300) in an attempt to kick-start the economy. Some UK commentators wondered why Brown could not do something similar. Well, now he has.

Just to be clear, 22 million people on the basic rate of tax — those earning under £35,000 — will receive an extra £120 this year. They will get £60 in September, and £10 a month after that.

Top rate tax payers will not benefit. But neither will they be penalised to pay for the pay cut — Darling is funding the tax cut through borrowing.

Source: www.guardian.co.uk

### Extract 2 Using the Budget to make it easy to go green

Friends of the Earth, which is calling on the Chancellor to deliver on his promise to put sustainability at the heart of his forthcoming Budget, has produced a blueprint for a green Budget. It outlines a variety of measures that Mr Darling must adopt to help the UK to develop a low-carbon economy, including a windfall tax on energy companies to finance a £5 billion Climate Change Super-Fund to kick start a programme to help eliminate fuel poverty, and a £10 billion tax shift programme raising taxes on pollution and cutting taxes on income, jobs and people.

Friends of the Earth's Economics Co-ordinator Simon Bullock said: 'Carbon dioxide emissions have risen under Labour. We've had enough of half measures and green spin. The Chancellor must put climate change at the heart of next week's Budget and make it cheaper and easier for people to go green.'

Source: www.foe.co.uk Friends of the Earth website

(a) Explain what is meant by the term 'fiscal policy'.                          (6 marks)

(b) With reference to Extract 1:
    (i)   Using an appropriate diagram, analyse how the £2.7 billion tax change outlined in the Extract may be used to 'kick start the economy'.                          (16 marks)
    (ii)   Assess the likely impact on the distribution of income in the UK which will result from the tax changes.                          (14 marks)

(c) With reference to Extracts 1 and 2, examine one way in which fiscal policy may be used to incorporate environmental goals.                          (14 marks)

*(d) Discuss the likely effect of changes in fiscal policy for the decisions on monetary policy made by the Monetary Policy Committee. Consider both the short and the long run in your response.                          (30 marks)

## Candidate's answer

(a) The government's manipulation of its spending (G) and taxation (T) in order to affect aggregate demand. Fiscal policy decisions are made by the government in the budget in March, although some further changes are often made in the autumn in the Pre-Budget Report. Fiscal policy can be used to achieve a variety of policy objectives, mainly economic growth, employment, and the distribution of income. Increasingly, in the views of some economists, fiscal policy has included 'green taxes' as a means to prevent further environmental problems.

If government spending is increased relative to taxation, then fiscal policy is said to be expansionary and *AD* shifts to the right. If government spending is increased at a slower rate than taxation, then fiscal policy is said to be **contractionary**.

**6/6 marks**

Accurate answers such as this earn full marks.

**4**

**question**

**(b) (i)** Kick starting the economy implies that the government is aiming to increase output and spending. This can be shown by a movement to the right on the real output axis.

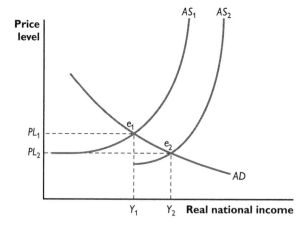

The increase in government spending of £2.7 billion will increase aggregate demand. Price levels will increase and output will increase. There will be a multiplier effect, which is the knock on effect when an injection such as $G$ increases while $T$ stays constant.

There will also be an impact on the supply side of the economy. If people are paying less tax there will be an incentive to work harder for those already in work, and those who are not in the workforce (the economically inactive) will have an increased incentive to join the workforce. As the workforce increases, wages will be bid downwards and the economy becomes more competitive. **13/16 marks**

📝 The analysis is exceptionally good because both the demand and the supply side are considered. It is always advisable to mention the multiplier when discussing an *AD* shift, as is done here. However the shift in *AD* is incorrect (it is shown by a left rather than a rightward shift). It would also be better to incorporate both shifts on one diagram to show the overall effects on output, with both of the shifts increasing the equilibrium real output. It is odd that different labels are used on the horizontal axis for what is meant to represent the same thing. Therefore, full marks would not be earned for the diagrams they would only receive 1 out of the 4 marks available.

**(b) (ii)**  In general a tax windfall like this is likely to help lower income groups by a larger proportion than higher income groups. Therefore the distribution of income will 'improve' in the sense that inequalities are reduced. However this masks some of the picture.

In Extract 1 it is stated that standard rate tax payers will gain by £120 a year, but this will not affect top rate tax payers. Actually this is wrong, because top rate tax payers do also pay standard rate tax on some of their income. While it will affect the distribution of income (lower income groups will see a higher proportional benefit) it is not exactly as the author makes out. Furthermore, at the other end of the income distribution, people who don't have any work at all will not gain the £120 and therefore the distribution of income will widen. **14/14 marks**

The analysis is secure, because two groups are identified, and the relative change in income for these groups is described. The evaluation is also highly awarded because the candidate pulls out a major inaccuracy in the data. Clearly top rate taxpayers will get the £120 benefit too. However this level of analysis is not expected at AS level Unit 2 and so while the marks will be awarded the point is unlikely to appear on the official mark scheme. Other ways to evaluate would be to say that the increased government borrowing will have to be paid back at some point, and it is not clear which part of the population will pay that. In addition, other things are not equal. Lower income taxes might attract more investment from abroad which might mean more job opportunities for people in Britain. More demand for workers will make wages rise.

**(c)**  Green taxes can be used as part of fiscal policy. This is where the main aim of the policy is not to change *AD* but to change the way in which spending occurs so that carbon dioxide emissions are reduced. One obvious way to do this is to increase the tax on petrol. Of course no one likes paying more, but the net effect on consumer disposable income need not change overall because the government could spend more on public services such as transport. In Extract 2 this is called a '£10 billion tax shift programme', and the emphasis is on changing the way in which taxes are imposed and not the overall tax burden.

In my view the cost of petrol is already far too high, and most of the journeys that are made are necessary to the way our economy works. In other words, demand is price inelastic because the public services are total rubbish. Trains are overcrowded and buses only go along the main, congested routes and never at times to suit demand. If the private sector was running the transport system it might not be any better, but I can't see how throwing money at the public sector is going to help. You can't have more trains running on the Underground; it's already at full capacity. Transport is the main thing stifling productivity growth in the UK, and green taxes are not going to help. **10/14 marks**

> The good thing about this answer is that it uses the passage, describes how green taxes would work, and goes on to evaluate. The bad thing is that the comments are rather over enthusiastic in rhetoric, and measured analysis is the opportunity cost here. Rather than using words such as 'rubbish' and 'of course', more effort could be put into offering a viable solution.

**(d)** The MPC considers an enormous range of data when coming to a decision on the interest rate. It looks at pressures in the labour market, housing market, commodity prices, external exchange and the global economy, to name but a few. The fiscal stance is also of great interest to the MPC. If the government is seen as operating a loose fiscal policy as outlined in Extract 1, the MPC might consider the impact on the real side of the economy and on the money markets. Government spending has to be financed and if it is not going to be financed by taxation then the money has to come from somewhere. In this case it is by borrowing. It is the extent to which borrowing affects inflationary pressures which is of concern to the MPC. The MPC has only one objective: to maintain the inflation target. Therefore any softness by the government in its fiscal policy is likely to be compensated for by tight monetary policy — that is a raising of interest rates.

The borrowing can have two very different effects on inflationary pressures. If there is spare capacity in the economy then expansionary fiscal policy can cause some increased growth without damaging inflationary pressures. If there is no spare capacity — that is, full employment — then there will be inflation. This can be shown using an *AS* curve, and as the elasticity falls (the *AS* curve gets steeper), the inflationary pressures increase.

There is a similar set of opposites in the money markets. If there is plenty of credit around then extra government borrowing will not have much effect on the cost of credit. But in times of the 'credit crunch' when it is hard to get loans and inter-bank loans are at high interest rates then increased borrowing will crowd out the market. In this case, government expansion will not be inflationary, and will merely tighten the monetary side of the economy.

In conclusion, it is difficult to say how the MPC will react to expansionary fiscal policy. It depends entirely on the context. If there is spare capacity in the economy and there is plenty of available credit then it is unlikely to react. But in the case where bottlenecks are appearing and prices are edging upwards, the MPC might raise rates. If the money market is short of credit, however, this might not be needed as increased cost of credit will in itself control aggregate demand and therefore restrain inflationary pressures. **28/30 marks**

🖉 This is a sophisticated response, on what is probably the most challenging part of the specification. The only noticeable weakness is the absence of a diagram, although the shape of the AS curve is described well. A simple sketch to illustrate the bottlenecks in supply would earn 4/4 diagram marks rather than the two earned from the attempt at a describing this.

**Total score: 71/80 = grade A**